Our Path for His Glory

Kimmy Kay Serafy

All Bible verses quoted throughout the text are taken from the King James Version of the Holy Bible, unless otherwise noted.

Cover photograph of Rachel and Eric Davis was taken in Puerto Rico, by the author, Kimmy Kay Serafy.

Printed in the United States of America

Facebook
Kim Serafy Author
@KimmyKaySerafy

ISBN: 9781676471134

~Dedication

To Rachel, Keith, and Joel. I am humbled, and very thankful to be your Mama. The greatest privilege I have ever been blessed with, was staying home to raise and homeschool the three of you. What an honor it was to teach you about the love that Jesus has for you. I pray that you walk in the abundant love, grace, and mercy that Jesus extends to you. I love you more than words could ever express.

TABLE OF CONTENTS

~Preface

The motivation behind writing this book stemmed from my desire to help others, as well as myself, better understand the dynamics of our relationship with God. Additionally, I sincerely believe that it is critical that we are firmly rooted in The Word of God and prayer. We must keep our hearts and minds stayed on Christ. As a result, we will experience the Holy Spirit manifesting Himself in and through us. He will provide power that sustains us throughout our life's journey. My prayer is that this book will be a tool that is useful in strengthening your relationship with our Lord and Savior, Jesus Christ.

Our intentions should never be to maintain a stagnant, underdeveloped relationship with anyone whom we love, especially Jesus. My prayer is that this book acts as a catalyst for spiritual growth and enrichment. No personal endeavor should be prioritized above cultivating our relationship with God. Our main purpose is to bring glory and honor to our Lord and Savior, Jesus Christ.

Through careful study of God's Word and dedication to His plan and purpose, we can expect our relationship with the Lord to blossom. I pray that your daily Bible study, along with the addition of these studies, will help cultivate your spiritual growth. Moreover, I pray that there will be an increase in your adoration of our Lord and Savior, Jesus Christ. I pray that as a result of reading through this collection of Bible studies, you will begin to long for, appreciate, and anticipate all that God has planned for you.

As the words jump from the pages, and into your heart and mind, you will see a transformation of your thoughts. Expect a renewal of your heart's posture toward God. I pray that your heart and mind remains stayed on Christ. Ready yourself to experience all that God has for you. Prepare your heart and mind to receive from the Lord, as you study His Word. Prepare your heart and mind to receive from the Lord, as you read the studies prepared for you throughout this book.

I have one goal in my writing, and that is to see Christ glorified. I praise God for the privilege of seeing this through. I am grateful, as well as humbled, that you are reading the words that the Lord has inspired me to put on paper. I pray that you will find hope, encouragement, and truth, as you read, study, and pray.

In Christ,

Kimmy Kay

Our Path for His Glory

~ Part One

Part One is composed of daily studies that are designed to instruct, encourage, and promote a better understanding of the depth of God's love for us. I pray that you will better understand the love God has for us, what Jesus did, and what He continues to do for those who place their faith and trust in Him. My prayer is that as you read, you will develop an appropriate perspective of what a consecrated, or set apart, life of trust, faith, and obedience looks like. With understanding and application of the Word of God, our lives will fall into alignment with the will of God. There is no other relationship that should be prioritized above our relationship with Jesus. As He draws you towards Himself, forever linger in His presence. You will see that there is no better place to dwell.

~ Salvation: Freely Given

It would be foolish of me to assume that everyone reading these writings has a personal relationship with our Lord and Savior, Jesus Christ. Most, if not all people, at some point, wonder why we are even here on Earth. Most have questioned the purpose of our existence. Many who are told that they are sinners, and that they are in need of salvation, wonder what that even means. Many questions go unanswered, and people remain unsaved, and bound to their sin. What is our purpose here on earth? Why do we need to be saved? What are we being saved from? Who saves us? What is the result of our salvation?

We are here on earth purposefully, without question, to give glory and honor to God. There is one God. He is our creator. He is Holy, and He created us in His image. He created us to be in fellowship with Him. When we place our faith and trust in Jesus, He saves us from the penalty for our sin. He sustains us. He protects us. He gives us purpose. He secures our place with Him for all eternity. Salvation is much more than being saved from going to Hell.

We must first deny the spirit of unbelief that is so prevalent in our culture. We are not here by accident, nor by coincidence. We are here because God created us. In fact, God created everything that has been created. Colossians 1: 16-17 says, "For by him were all things created, that are in heaven, and that are in earth, visible and invisible, whether they be thrones, or dominions, or principalities, or powers: all things were created by him, and for him: And he is before all things, and by him all things consist." He created us, and He diligently pursues our hearts.

We are all restless and rebellious by nature, and in need of God's presence in our lives. You might ask, "Why are we considered restless and rebellious?" We are considered rebellious because God created us to glorify Him. As a result of our sin nature, we go our own way. Our failure to submit to the will and ways of the Lord, results in restlessness in our souls. Our restlessness began shortly after God created man. God created Adam and Eve, and they lived in perfect harmony with God. God created them with free will, and they chose to listen to the devil, and they rebelled against God.

The devil was an angel that rebelled against God. This was before the creation of man. The devil wanted to be equal with God. He was cast out of heaven because of his pride, and has tormented mankind with his deceptive ways since Adam and Eve. The devil deceived Adam and Eve, into doubting what God had told them. They fell for the devil's lies. As a result, sin and rebellion have been woven into the DNA of mankind ever since.

We are no different than Adam and Eve. We each go our own way. Isaiah 53:6 tells us, "All we like sheep have gone astray; we have turned everyone to his own way; and the LORD hath laid on him the iniquity of us all."

Despite our disobedience, God still persistently pursues our hearts. He is continually chasing after us, to draw us to Him. His desire for us is to know Him, and to place our faith and trust in Him alone. God loves us all.

It is because of God's great love for us, that He sent Jesus as payment, in full, for all of our sin. That includes past, current, and future sin. We are all bound by our sin until we submit our lives to Jesus. No one is exempt from requiring deliverance. We all must be born again. In John 3:3 Jesus says, "Jesus answered and said unto him, Verily, verily, I say unto thee, except a man be born again, he cannot see the kingdom of God."

Salvation is the act of Jesus delivering us, or rescuing us from the penalty for our sin. Salvation is the amazingly, unmerited, free gift, only obtained through Jesus, from God. Salvation is more than assurance of eternal life in heaven. Salvation brings hope, joy, and freedom.

Sin is anything that does not please God. Sin is what keeps us far from God. Let's face it, we are stubborn, and we think we know best. His desire is for us to be reconciled with Him, but our pride prevents us from saying yes to the plans He has for us. Each of us must come to an authentic understanding and acceptance of the saving grace of Jesus Christ. His plans for us are unique, individual, and perfectly suited for each of us. We must decide to yield to God's authority, and allow Him to guide and direct our paths.

Jeremiah 29:11-13 asserts, "For I know the thoughts that I think toward you, saith the Lord, thoughts of peace, and not of evil, to give you an expected end. Then shall ye call upon me, and ye shall go and pray unto me, and I will hearken unto you. And ye shall seek me, and find me, when ye shall search for me with all your heart." God patiently waits for us to recognize our need for Him, and ushers us into His presence when we commit our lives to Him.

God can have nothing to do with our sin. Romans 6:23 tells us, "For the wages of sin is death; but the gift of God is eternal life through Jesus Christ our Lord." Before Jesus, sins had to be paid for through an animal sacrifice. This was something that God required before anyone could enter into His presence. We all have sinned against God. God prepared a perfect plan of redemption for mankind. He put an end to repetitive animal blood sacrifices. He sent Jesus to be the one and only payment needed for our sin.

Jesus, who is fully God, was made flesh, and dwelt among men. He was sent to earth as a baby, born of a virgin. He grew up and became the final sacrifice for the sin of all mankind. He laid down His life, and was raised to life on the third day. After His death, burial, and resurrection, there was no longer a need for another sin sacrifice. John 3:16 says, "For God so loved the world, that he gave his only begotten Son, that whosoever believeth in him should not perish, but have everlasting life." Jesus is the way for us to be saved from the penalty for our sin.

Jesus has bridged the gap between us and God. He has made a way for us to have full and direct access to Him. Ephesians 2:8 says, "For by grace are ye saved through faith; and that not of yourselves: it is the gift of God." In fact, there is nothing we have to do. Christ did it all, on our behalf. We must believe, by faith, and receive God's gift of salvation through Jesus Christ. It is that simple. This simple act of obedience will change your life, and save you from the penalty of sin. It saves you from living in spiritual darkness. It saves you from spiritual death and separation from God.

God is patient, because He knows the turmoil that sin causes in our lives. He knew that creating us with free will would create barriers for us to overcome, in order for us to choose Him. He does not want us to be His puppets, who are forced to follow Him. He wants us to willingly choose Him. He wants us to be able to freely choose life over death. It does not matter how nice, good, thankful, rich, generous, or caring you are. If you haven't made Jesus the Lord of your life, you are going to Hell. Once you are dead, there is no other opportunity to receive salvation.

Our free will affords us the ability to make our own choices. At the same time, we must also own the consequences of those choices. Galatians 6: 7-8 warns, "Be not deceived; God is not mocked: for whatsoever a man soweth, that shall he also reap. For he that soweth to his flesh shall of the flesh reap corruption; but he that soweth to the Spirit shall of the Spirit reap life everlasting." Whatever choice we make for eternity, it will be ours and ours alone.

God has given mankind the power to choose our own eternal destination. We can choose a relationship with Him, which leads to peace, hope, and everlasting life in heaven. The alternative, is choosing to reject God, which leads to eternal separation from Him. In essence, it is our choice how we live our lives on earth, and it is our choice where we will spend eternity.

We are desperately in need of salvation, in need of redemption, and in need of freedom from the penalty for our sin. These needs can only be met through placing our faith and trust in Jesus Christ. Ephesians 1:7 tells us, "In whom we have redemption through his blood, the forgiveness of sins, according to the riches of his grace." God sent Jesus, His only begotten son to earth in human form. He lived among us. He was crucified. He was buried. He rose on the third day. He did it all for us.

God created us in His likeness. Because He created us to be united with Him, we have a void in our lives when our lives are not in alignment with His will. We spend much of our time trying to fill that void with things other than Him. Because of this, that void is never permanently satisfied or fulfilled. It isn't until we surrender our will for His, and ask

Jesus into our lives, that the void is filled. This decision for Christ brings freedom, peace, and newness of life. Jesus is a life-changer, and makes every crooked place straight. Will you trust Him for it?

When we place our faith and trust in Jesus, and in what He did for us, the trajectory of our lives instantly changes. We are made new in Christ. II Corinthians 5:17 promises, "Therefore if any man be in Christ, he is a new creature: old things are passed away; behold, all things are become new." If this is what you are longing for, if this is what you have been missing, if you want Jesus in your life, then call upon His name.

Tell Jesus you believe He is who He says He is. Ask Jesus to forgive you for going your own way. Ask God, in Jesus' name, to save you from the penalty for your sins, and cleanse you of all unrighteousness. Done.

Romans 10:13 says, "For whosoever shall call upon the name of the Lord shall be saved."

Draw near to God, and keep your heart and mind stayed on Him.

~Prophecy Of Christ's Birth

Throughout the Old Testament of the Bible, Christ's birth, life, death, and resurrection are foreshadowed. Let's come to a greater understanding and appreciation of what Christ did for us at Calvary.

Most people have at least heard the story of the birth of Christ: that He was born in a manger, because there was no room at the Inn. Not everyone has heard, nor understands, the foretelling of Jesus Christ's birth, His actual birth, His ministry on earth, His death, His resurrection, and His ascension into heaven. There is so much to know and appreciate about our Lord and Savior, Jesus Christ.

The entire Bible is about Jesus. The story of our Savior unfolds throughout the pages of Scripture, from Genesis to Revelation. The Old Testament was written hundreds of years before the birth of Jesus, but there are numerous prophecies concerning Him. Let's look at some of the prophecies in Isaiah, foretelling the virgin birth of Jesus. Isaiah was a prophet who lived several hundred years before Jesus was born. He foretold the future coming of the Messiah, Jesus Christ.

Because of the sin of Adam and Eve, all people born of natural conception are born with a sin nature. As a result, the one who would take away the sins of the world with His blood had to be born of a virgin. He is the Son of Almighty God, and at the same time, He is God. Isaiah foretold the birth of Christ, nearly seven hundred years before Jesus was born.

Isaiah prophesies the virgin birth in Isaiah 7:14, when he says, "Therefore the Lord himself shall give you a sign; Behold, a virgin shall conceive, and bear a son, and shall call his name Immanuel." Isaiah 9:6 also says, "For unto us a child is born, unto us a son is given: and the government shall be upon his shoulder: and his name shall be called Wonderful, Counsellor, The mighty God, The everlasting Father, The Prince of Peace."

About Christ's birth, Isaiah 11:1 says, "And there shall come forth a rod out of the stem of Jesse, and a Branch shall grow out of his roots:" These prophetic words spoken by the prophet Isaiah, demonstrate that the birth of our Savior was no ordinary event. Jesus, being born of a virgin in order to reconcile us to God, was the work of Almighty God. God wanted it to be crystal clear: that this would be no ordinary birth for an extraordinary Savior.

It is important to see that the prophet Isaiah, who lived centuries before Jesus came to earth in human form, was given revelation of the future coming of a Savior. These prophecies were fulfilled exactly as they were given. Matthew 1:18 says, "Now the birth of Jesus Christ was on this wise: When as his mother Mary was espoused to Joseph, before they came together, she was found with child of the Holy Ghost."

Matthew 1:21-23 says, "And she shall bring forth a son, and thou shalt call his name Jesus: for he shall save his people from their sins. Now all this was done, that it might be fulfilled which was spoken of the Lord by the prophet, saying, Behold, a virgin shall be with child, and shall bring forth a son, and they shall call his name Emmanuel, which being interpreted is, God with us." Just as the prophecy was given to Isaiah centuries beforehand, so it was fulfilled.

Jesus is the second person of the trinity, who is fully God, and fully God's Son. He had to be placed in Mary's womb, by the Holy Spirit, so that He would remain perfect, and sinless. Jesus was not, and could not, be conceived naturally by man and woman. All humans, because of Adam's sin, are born with a sin nature woven into their DNA. He could not be tainted with sin. Therefore, He had to be placed in Mary's womb by God. He could not have a human father. I Peter 2:22 says, "Who (Jesus) did no sin, neither was guile found in his mouth:"

The prophecy of Christ's birth is critical. Thousands of years before His birth, the prophets spoke of His coming. From Genesis to Revelation, Christ is preached. Through the revelation of God, we see the preparations being made for the birth of the Savior of the world.

~The Birth Of Christ

The truth and validity of the Gospel is dependent on the profound miracle of the birth of Jesus. It is ultimately because of the birth of our Lord and Savior, Jesus Christ, that we have the option to choose eternity spent with Him. Without His birth, there would have been no death and resurrection. Without His birth, there would be no forgiveness for sins. The foundation for our faith, purpose, hope, and freedom is the birth of Jesus Christ.

Jesus was not an ordinary baby born of ordinary parents. Jesus was the manifestation of God in human form. John 1:14 tells us, "And the Word was made flesh, and dwelt among us, (and we beheld his glory, the glory as of the only begotten of the Father,) full of grace and truth." The Word is Jesus. John 1:1 says, "In the beginning was the Word, and the Word was with God, and the Word was God." Jesus has always been. He came to dwell among us, so He could fulfill God's will.

The Holy Trinity consists of God the Father, God the Son, and God the Holy Spirit. The three are all God, each in a different form. All have always been, with no beginning, and no end. God is Holy, and Adam and Eve's disobedience introduced sin into the world. Sin separates us from God. Romans 6:23 tells us, "For the wages of sin is death; but the gift of God is eternal life through Jesus Christ our Lord." God had determined that the wages of sin is death, so He needed a perfect sacrifice to atone for our sin.

The one who would pay the sin debt had to be sinless. God needed a one-time, sinless, atonement for all sin. Before Jesus, man's sin was atoned for with repeated animal sacrifices. God sent Jesus into the world, the sinless Son of God, to be the last and only permanent atonement for our sins. I John 2:2 says, "And he is the propitiation for our sins: and not for ours only, but also for the sins of the whole world."

God the Father sent God the son into the world to be the perfect sinless sacrifice. This was done to save those who place their faith and trust in Him, from eternal separation from God. Paul says in I Timothy 1:15, "This is a faithful saying, and worthy of all acceptation, that Christ Jesus came into the world to save sinners; of whom I am chief." The Holy Spirit placed Jesus into the womb of Mary to be born into the world. Jesus was not only fully human, but also fully God. He simultaneously was perfectly Holy and human. He was untainted by sin, because He did not have an earthly father.

God masterfully executed the impregnation and birth of Jesus Christ. It may seem difficult to wrap our human minds around, but the reality is that Mary gave birth to God the Son. The reality is that God became man. The reality is that Jesus Christ's birth was the literal incarnation of God.

Jesus's birth began our path to everlasting freedom. His birth demonstrated God's relentless pursuit of our hearts, providing the only way for mankind to be reconciled to Him. Jesus was born in human flesh, for us. The birth of Jesus Christ, our Lord and Savior, was and is the greatest gift ever bestowed upon mankind. What a mighty God we serve: overflowing with love, mercy, and grace toward us.

~The Ministry Of Jesus Christ

All of the events of Jesus' birth and ministry occurred in order to draw men to Him. It was all a demonstration of God's love for us.

Jesus humbled Himself, became human, and lived among us. I John 4:9 says, "In this was manifested the love of God toward us, because that God sent his only begotten Son into the world, that we might live through him." God placed Jesus on earth, in human form, to teach, preach, love, heal, and save. He was placed here to satisfy the plans and purposes of Almighty God. His purpose on earth was to save the lost, serve, give His life as payment for sin, preach the good news, and ultimately turn the hearts of mankind to God.

His purpose was, and still is, to reconcile mankind back to God. He is the bridge, that closes the gap that sin causes between God and man. In Matthew 5:17, Jesus says, "Think not that I am come to destroy the law, or the prophets: I am not come to destroy, but to fulfil." He came to earth, to fulfill the law and the prophets, so that mankind could be reconciled with God.

Jesus most likely had a pretty normal infancy and early childhood. He did not have to wrestle with His own sin, like we do, because He was the sinless Son of God. Jesus wasted no time establishing His earthly ministry. Luke 2:40 tells us,

"And the child grew, and waxed strong in spirit, filled with wisdom: and the grace of God was upon him." When Jesus was a twelve-year-old boy, He and His parents went to Jerusalem for the annual Passover feast.

When they left to go back home, His parents did not realize that He was not with them. Luke 2:40 says, "And it came to pass, that after three days they found him in the temple, sitting in the midst of the doctors, both hearing them, and asking them questions." His response in Luke 2:49 says, "And he said unto them, how is it that ye sought me? wist ye not that I must be about my Father's business?" He continued to grow and mature, until He began His earthly ministry. Luke 2:52 tells us, "And Jesus increased in wisdom and stature, and in favor with God and man."

Jesus began His adult ministry at around the age of thirty. Matthew 4:23 tells us, "And Jesus went about all Galilee, teaching in their synagogues, and preaching the gospel of the kingdom, and healing all manner of sickness and all manner of disease among the people." Jesus came preaching and teaching in a manner of obedience and service. He came with God's message of repentance, but with a heart's posture of love, mercy, patience, grace, compassion, and forgiveness. John 3:17 says, "For God sent not his Son into the world to condemn the world; but that the world through him might be saved."

Jesus was met with fierce opposition and resistance from the religious leaders of the day. These obstacles did not hinder Jesus from fulfilling His appointed mission. In Luke 4:18 Jesus says, "The Spirit of the Lord is upon me, because he hath anointed me to preach the gospel to the poor; he hath sent me to heal the brokenhearted, to preach deliverance to the captives, and recovering of sight to the blind, to set at liberty them that are bruised."

Jesus spent His time teaching in parables, preaching sermons, and performing miracles. In Mark 1:38 Jesus says, "And he said unto them, let us go into the next towns, that I may preach there also: for therefore came I forth." He spent most of His time with the disciples and sinners.

Jesus spent much of His time teaching Biblical life lessons through parables. Jesus told dozens of parables, which are stories to illustrate Biblical truths. When we read the four Gospels (Matthew, Mark, Luke, and John), we get very familiar with Jesus and His fervent love for all people. He desired to pour into people, that they may come to know the love that God has for them. The Gospel message still comes to life as we read it today.

Jesus taught lessons to guide our lives through parables. Mark 4:34 says, "But without a parable spake he not unto them: and when they were alone, he expounded all things to his disciples." Jesus would always explain the parables to the disciples afterwards. In Mark 4:9 Jesus says, "And he said unto them, He that hath ears to hear, let him hear." In Matthew 13:13 Jesus says, "Therefore speak I to them in parables: because they seeing see not; and hearing they hear not, neither do they understand." Jesus desired that all would hear with spiritual ears, knowing that we choose what we want to hear. We must desire to hear the Word of Truth.

Jesus also taught by delivering sermons throughout the Gospels. Sermons are talks, or speeches, on spiritual and Biblical topics. These were not parables, but pure Biblical preaching. Jesus gave several sermons, but none of them as lengthy as The Sermon on the Mount found in the book of Matthew. This can be found in chapters five through seven.

The people of Jesus' time did not have the New Testament to read and understand about salvation, and the blood of Jesus that would be shed to redeem us. He was walking amongst the people living out the Gospel in real time. Many were plagued by the spirit of unbelief. Jesus performed Miracles as a visible testimony of who He was. People were more likely to believe if He performed the supernatural before their eyes. Jesus healed the sick, restored vision, raised the dead to life, turned water into wine, and so on.

The greatest miracle of all was His own resurrection. Matthew 28:5-6 says, "And the angel answered and said unto the women, Fear not ye: for I know that ye seek Jesus, which was crucified. He is not here: for he is risen, as he said. Come, see the place where the Lord lay." We will discuss this at a later time.

Jesus was sinless, and although He faced all of the same struggles and temptations as we do, He never sinned. He was able to overcome it all, because He lived the flawless, sinless life of obedience. He was God in the flesh. John 1:14 says, "And the Word was made flesh, and dwelt among us, (and we beheld his glory, the glory as of the only begotten of the Father,) full of grace and truth."

His entire ministry on earth was spent drawing mankind to Himself. He taught Godly principles of repentance, forgiveness, love, mercy, and grace. He poured Himself out, so that many would be saved. Jesus displayed God's love for us. He lived the Gospel message: to save the lost. He did all of it, knowing that He would have to suffer a terrible death to atone for our sins, and reconcile us to God. God's love for us is supernatural. His love for us is flawless.

~The Last Supper

We have studied the Old Testament prophecy of the birth of Jesus, the actual birth of Jesus, the ministry of Jesus, and now we will discuss The Last Supper.

The Last Supper was the last meal, and gathering for fellowship, that Jesus engaged in with His disciples before He was arrested and crucified. The account of the Last Supper is described in detail in the Gospels of Matthew, Mark, and Luke, in the Holy Bible.

Jesus had fulfilled His earthly mission, and He would share the Last Supper, and what we now call Holy Communion, with His disciples before His death. Matthew 26:19-20 says, "And the disciples did as Jesus had appointed them; and they made ready the Passover. Now when the even was come, he sat down with the twelve."

During the last supper, Jesus exposed the one who would betray Him. Judas Iscariot had already arranged to betray Jesus, and turn Him over to the Roman soldiers. He was simply waiting for the right opportunity. Matthew 26:14-16 says, "Then one of the twelve, called Judas Iscariot, went unto the chief priests, and said unto them, What will ye give me, and I will deliver him unto you? And they covenanted with him for thirty pieces of silver. And from that time he sought opportunity to betray him." God has always been in control, and He wasn't going to stop now.

This was Judas' God appointed opportunity. As Jesus and the twelve sat down for the meal, Jesus exposed Judas, as the one who would betray Him. Matthew 26:23 says, "And he answered and said, He that dippeth his hand with me in the dish, the same shall betray me." As tragic as it was, all of the events were still very much under God's mighty hand of authority.

A marvelous illustration took place during the last supper, when Jesus broke bread, and drank with the disciples. This intimate action was done, to indicate further, what was soon going to take place. Matthew 26: 26-28 tells us, "And as they were eating, Jesus took bread, and blessed it, and brake it, and gave it to the disciples, and said, Take, eat; this is my body. And he took the cup, and gave thanks, and gave it to them, saying, Drink ye all of it; For this is my blood of the new testament, which is shed for many for the remission of sins." Jesus' words were spoken with love, expectation, forgiveness, and hope.

Jesus took the bread, broke it, and shared it with His disciples. This was to symbolize His body, broken for us. There was so much humility, grace, and mercy in His sacrifice. The drink, represented His shed blood, poured out to atone for our sins. We did absolutely nothing to deserve this gift of life at the expense of His. This is Grace.

God displayed His favor that He has lavished on us through Christ's death. This is favor. This is Grace. Jesus stepped down from Heaven, joined mankind, and spilled His blood; all so that we do not have to receive the punishment for our sin, that we deserve. This is Mercy.

The Last supper was perfectly orchestrated to take place around the time of the celebrated Passover. Luke 22:8 says,

"And he sent Peter and John, saying, Go and prepare us the Passover, that we may eat." Recall the plague of death over Egypt, when God spared the Israelites. Exodus 12:12-14 tells us, "For I will pass through the land of Egypt this night, and will smite all the firstborn in the land of Egypt, both man and beast; and against all the gods of Egypt I will execute judgment: I am the Lord. And the blood shall be to you for a token upon the houses where ye are: and when I see the blood, I will pass over you, and the plague shall not be upon you to destroy you, when I smite the land of Egypt. And this day shall be unto you for a memorial; and ye shall keep it a feast to the Lord throughout your generations; ye shall keep it a feast by an ordinance forever."

In Exodus, it was a lamb's blood that saved all of the firstborn of God's people. Jesus shed his blood to save us from the penalty of sin, which is spiritual death. If we ask Jesus to be Lord of our Lives, His blood will erase our sin debt. He did it all for us. One sacrifice, as the payment for sin, was extended to all who believe on His name.

Jesus: He is our Passover lamb.

~Jesus Is Apprehended

Our Lord and Savior, Jesus Christ, was despised and rejected by so many. He was revered by some, but for the most part, He was hated by those who refused to believe. Many were looking for a different kind of messiah, and had blinded eyes and bitter souls. Isaiah 53 paints a beautiful picture of the love Jesus has for us, that He would suffer so severely on our behalf.

Isaiah 53:3 says, "He is despised and rejected of men; a man of sorrows, and acquainted with grief: and we hid as it were our faces from him; he was despised, and we esteemed him not." He knew Judas was going to turn Him over. He knew that soon after He left the upper room, He would be apprehended. He knew He would face extreme ridicule. He knew He would be beaten. He knew He would die a gruesome death. He knew. He could have stopped everything, at any moment, because He is God. His love for us is so intense that He endured.

Jesus never stopped preaching repentance, salvation available for all, and the love of God. He was well aware of everything that would happen to Him, but it never deterred Him from manifesting the Gospel through His life. That is the Jesus we serve.

Recall, Jesus was placed on earth as a human, and even though He was without sin, He still expressed emotions. He was apprehensive about what was about to happen, because He knew that it was going to be brutal. He prayed three times after the Last Supper, and before His arrest, that if it was God's will, He would prefer not to go through with His assignment on earth.

He had asked the disciples to pray, while He was seeking God in prayer, but they kept falling asleep. Matthew 26:39 records, "And he went a little farther, and fell on his face, and prayed, saying, O my Father, if it be possible, let this cup pass from me: nevertheless, not as I will, but as thou wilt." Again, Matthew 26:42 says, "He went away again the second time, and prayed, saying, O my Father, if this cup may not pass away from me, except I drink it, thy will be done." Lastly, Matthew 26:44 says, "And he left them, and went away again, and prayed the third time, saying the same words." Although Jesus had feelings of trepidation about these final events, He remained committed.

For three years, Jesus peacefully walked the streets, shared the gospel, healed the sick and demon possessed, and more. He never posed a threat to anyone. Yet, when it was time to arrest Him, they came as though they were arresting a violent, disorderly criminal. Matthew 26:47 says, "And while he yet spake, lo, Judas, one of the twelve, came, and with him a great multitude with swords and staves, from the chief priests and elders of the people."

Judas led the Roman soldiers to Jesus. Matthew 26: 48-49 tells us, "Now he that betrayed him gave them a sign, saying, Whomsoever I shall kiss, that same is he: hold him fast. And forthwith he came to Jesus, and said, Hail, master; and kissed him." They seized Jesus, as though He were a criminal. Jesus never resisted.

Jesus was still fully composed with peace and love. Matthew 26:55 says, "In that same hour said Jesus to the multitudes, are ye come out as against a thief with swords and staves for to take me? I sat daily with you teaching in the temple, and ye laid no hold on me." Jesus did not resist, for this was the will of God. Jesus was fully committed to providing the final atonement for our sins.

If Jesus wanted to, He easily could have changed the storyline, but He knew that this was the best for mankind. This was the greatest display of mercy and grace. Matthew 26:53-54 says, "Thinkest thou that I cannot now pray to my Father, and he shall presently give me more than twelve legions of angels? But how then shall the scriptures be fulfilled, that thus it must be?" Jesus' love for us is so grand, so deep, and so sacrificial, that He peacefully went with the Roman soldiers.

Jesus was taken to court. Matthew 26:57 says, "And they that had laid hold on Jesus led him away to Caiaphas the high priest, where the scribes and the elders were assembled." The chief priests, elders, and all the council tried to produce false testimony concerning Jesus. No one had anything concrete to hold against Jesus.

He remained quiet throughout all of the prodding, but then they insisted that He answer them. When asked if He is the Christ, the Son of God, He said, "I Am." Matthew 26:65 says, "Then the high priest rent his clothes, saying, He hath spoken blasphemy; what further need have we of witnesses? behold, now ye have heard his blasphemy." Their hearts and minds were blinded to Truth, and they were overcome by a spirit of disbelief.

Following the arrest of Jesus, all of the disciples abandoned Him. At the Last Supper, Jesus told Peter that after the cock would crow three times, he will have denied Jesus three times.

It happened, just as He said it would. How lonely He must have felt. Our Savior was found guilty, although He was innocent. He was blamed, although blameless. He was silent. He never objected, and He never defended Himself. He was fulfilling His assignment for us.

~Our Real Names Are Barabbas

Jesus, who is fully God, was born of a virgin, to one day die on behalf of all mankind. God the Son walked the earth for over thirty years, knowing that this day would come. He knew the purpose of His coming. He came to earth, fully God and fully human, to die a gruesome death. All of this, in order to restore mankind's relationship with God.

Jesus finished the Last Supper with His disciples, and made His way to the garden at Gethsemane. Jesus prayed there, and asked God to spare Him of what was to come. He knew exactly what was going to happen, and the pain He would have to endure. He prayed to God, and said, "not my will, but your will be done," Shortly thereafter, Jesus was apprehended.

It was the custom, at the Passover feast, for the governor to release one prisoner to the people. Matthew 27:15 says, "Now at that feast the governor was wont to release unto the people a prisoner, whom they would." Jesus, who was completely innocent, and who had never committed a single crime, stood before the officials, and the crowd. In addition to Jesus, another prisoner stood before the crowd, named Barabbas.

Barabbas was well known as a horrible criminal. Matthew 27:16-17 says, "And they had then a notable prisoner, called Barabbas. Therefore, when they were gathered together, Pilate said unto them, whom will ye that I release unto you? Barabbas, or Jesus which is called Christ?" Now, Barabbas deserved to be a prisoner. He was a notorious criminal.

Although Barabbas did not deserve to be set free, Matthew 27:20 tells us, "the chief priests and elders persuaded the multitudes that they should ask for Barabbas, and destroy Jesus." The crowd relentlessly shouted for Jesus to be crucified, and Barabbas to be set free.

Jesus, the sinless, Son of God, would pay the price for not only Barabbas's sin, but also for the sins of the entire human race. Barabbas received his freedom, his redemption, his release, and did nothing to earn it. Barabbas did nothing to earn his freedom, nor did he get what he deserved for his crimes. He was released, chains removed, and set free.

We, like Barabbas, can be absolved of the guilt, shame, and penalty for our sins if we surrender our lives to Christ. Christ took the penalty for the iniquities of Barabbas before He died for the sins of the world. Barabbas, is a reminder of who we are, because of what Christ did for us. We have our freedom; he was also freed. We do not have to pay the penalty for our sins, Barabbas did not pay for his either.

We are born with a sin nature, and the penalty for sin is death. Romans 6:23 says, "For the wages of sin is death; but the gift of God is eternal life through Jesus Christ our Lord." We rightly deserve death, which is separation from God, for all eternity. Because of Jesus showing mercy on us, He does not give us what we deserve.

Because of the mercy of God, if we place our faith and trust in Jesus, He wipes the slate clean. Our chains, that had us bound to our sin, fall off. We are set free from sin, and we no longer have to pay the penalty for our sin. We, like Barabbas, who was a perpetual criminal, get to live in freedom. Enjoy your freedom, and sin no more.

~The Crucifixion Of Our Lord

He willingly gave His life to rescue us from the penalty for our sin.

Our Savior suffered through an agonizing death, all for us. If we really stop to absorb the magnitude of Christ's suffering, which was all on our behalf, it is unfathomable. He not only suffered physically, but also mentally, emotionally, and spiritually. What He had to endure, He endured in the flesh, mind, and soul. Yes, He is fully God, but His time on earth was also spent as a man.

The sinless Son of God took all of the sins of mankind upon Himself simultaneously. He experienced spiritual death, so that we do not have to. There is no other love imaginable like the love God has for us. Isaiah 53: 7 tells us," He was oppressed, and he was afflicted, yet he opened not his mouth: he is brought as a lamb to the slaughter, and as a sheep before her shearers is dumb, so he openeth not his mouth." He suffered through it all, because of His great love for us.

Jesus knew that He was innocent. He knew that this would be the course of events. He knew the suffering that would soon be His. He did not defend Himself. Jesus stood before the governor, Pilate, and was silent. He knew His purpose, and He was willing to pay our sin debt. He was going to fulfill His purpose for becoming human.

The crowd had a choice to release one prisoner, but they insisted that it not be Jesus. They hollered out that they wanted Jesus to be crucified. Matthew 27:20 says, "But the chief priests and elders persuaded the multitude that they should ask Barabbas, and destroy Jesus." Pilate released Barabbas, and the soldiers incessantly beat Jesus, before giving Him over to be crucified.

Jesus felt every beating, and every piercing, that was delivered to His body. His heart felt the pain of all the rejection, torment, and mocking. Every soldier took part in the torturing of Jesus. Matthew 27:27 says, "Then the soldiers of the governor took Jesus into the common hall, and gathered unto him the whole band of soldiers." They beat Him beyond recognition. A crown of thorns was placed on our Lord's head.

They showed Jesus absolutely no mercy. And to think, it was all because of His mercy extended to us, that Jesus underwent torture unto death. After beating Him mercilessly, they found a man Simon, to carry His cross to Golgotha, which is where they crucified Jesus.

It wasn't enough that Jesus hung on the cross to die. The seething disdain expressed toward Jesus, after He was already sentenced to death, was appalling. In Matthew 27, verse 35 it says, "They parted my garments among them, and upon my vesture did they cast lots."

As Jesus hung on the cross, beaten beyond recognition, they persistently tormented and mocked Him. Matthew 27:40-43 says, "And saying, thou that destroyest the temple, and buildest it in three days, save thyself. If thou be the Son of God, come down from the cross. Likewise, also the chief priests mocking him, with the scribes and elders, said, He saved others; himself he cannot save. If he be the King of Israel, let him now come down from the cross, and we will believe him. He trusted in God; let him deliver him now, if he will have him: for he said, I am the Son of God." The torment never ceased.

Jesus died a very slow and painful death. As He was dying, every sin of mankind was placed upon Him. Jesus Christ, God in human flesh, who knew no sin, became sin. As He was nearing death, and in His last breaths, Matthew 27:46 says, "And about the ninth hour Jesus cried with a loud voice, saying, Eli, Eli, lama sabachthani? that is to say, My God, my God, why hast thou forsaken me?" Because God cannot have anything to do with sin, Jesus was removed from the presence of God in this moment.

It is hard to imagine, Jesus, who is holy, who is God, was separated from Himself. He was separated from God the Father, all that is perfect and holy, as He took on our sin. This was probably more excruciating, than the gruesome torture He experienced. This is mercy shown toward us. Mercy.

John 19:30 says, "When Jesus therefore had received the vinegar, he said, It is finished: and he bowed his head, and gave up the ghost." Our beloved Lord and Savior Jesus Christ, died a gruesome death, so that we might be saved. Matthew 27:51 tells us, "And, behold, the veil of the temple was rent in twain from the top to the bottom; and the earth did quake, and the rocks rent;" Because of the sacrifice Jesus made, it affords us the opportunity to be at peace with God, and also gives us direct access to Him.

The veil between us and God, no longer exists. His shed blood, was sufficient. His shed blood, was the last sacrifice ever needed. His shed blood, paid our sin debt.

We deserve the punishment for our sin, which is spiritual death, and eternal separation from God. Jesus took this upon Himself, so that we could receive life everlasting in Jesus' name. The only requirement is that we place our faith and trust in Jesus. Never again would another sin sacrifice need to be made.

I Peter 3:18 says, "For Christ also hath once suffered for sins, the just for the unjust, that he might bring us to God, being put to death in the flesh, but quickened by the Spirit:" Jesus died to atone for our sins, once for all. Let's live for Him; let's praise His name forever. He is worthy. Christ died, so we could live!

~Jesus Christ Is Alive

Jesus is alive! Let's celebrate the empty tomb of Christ, and the Truth of His resurrection, daily.

Praise Jesus! The bedrock of our faith is the resurrection of our Lord and Savior, Jesus Christ. All of our hope, all of our assurance, all of our peace, all of our purpose, everything, rests in the Truth of the resurrection of Jesus Christ. This pivotal phenomenon of His death, burial, and resurrection happened so that we could be saved from the penalty required for our sin.

Without the resurrection, Christ would not be trustworthy, and the Bible would just be a good book. Jesus is the focal point of the Bible, from Genesis to Revelation. The Old Testament pointed to Jesus, His death, and His resurrection. Jesus spoke of His resurrection several times. If it were not true, He would no longer be trustworthy, and the Bible wouldn't be either. I Corinthians 15:14 tells us, "And if Christ be not risen, then is our preaching vain, and your faith is also vain." We know that The Bible is Truth, and Jesus is alive forevermore.

God is sovereign, and His promises are Truth. Death is the penalty for sin. Life everlasting is our reward for trusting in Jesus. Death was temporary for Jesus. Everything that happened, and everything that happens, is under the control of our Almighty, Sovereign God. I Corinthians 15:3-4 says, "For I delivered unto you first of all that which I also received, how that Christ died for our sins according to the scriptures; And that he was buried, and that he rose again the third day according to the scriptures."

The body of Jesus was prepared for burial, as was the custom of the day. Afterward, every precaution and security was taken to ensure that no one had access to the body of Jesus. Matthew 27:66 tells us, "So they went, and made the sepulcher sure, sealing the stone, and setting a watch." Behold the visible truth that nothing could hold Jesus down; nothing could prevent the will of God from being fulfilled.

The power and authority of our Heavenly Father is evidenced in the resurrection of Jesus Christ. John 20:1-9 tells us, "The first day of the week cometh Mary Magdalene early, when it was yet dark, unto the sepulcher, and seeth the stone taken away from the sepulcher." After a great quake, the stone was rolled back, An Angel of the Lord sat upon the stone, and with fear, the guards "became as dead men." The Angel of The Lord spoke to Mary.

Matthew 28: 5-6 says, "And the angel answered and said unto the women, Fear not ye: for I know that ye seek Jesus, which was crucified. He is not here: for he is risen, as he said. Come, see the place where the Lord lay." Luke 24:10 says, "It was Mary Magdalene and Joanna, and Mary the mother of James, and other women that were with them, which told these things unto the apostles."

Jesus made appearances to many after His resurrection. Many did not even realize that He was in their midst, even as they talked about what had happened to Him. They did not recognize Him. Luke 24:32 says, "And they said one to another, did not our heart burn within us, while he talked with us by the way, and while he opened to us the scriptures?" Some, upon realizing that Jesus did arise from the dead, were fearful, or filled with unbelief. Luke 24:40 tells us, "And when he had thus spoken, he shewed them his hands and his feet." He spent forty days on earth after His resurrection.

It was important for Jesus to be seen. It was important that the people who trusted in Him could see Him alive. It was equally important for those who did not trust in him, to see Him alive. The testimony concerning Him was in fact Truth. He spent those weeks following His resurrection erasing doubt. His resurrected body further demonstrated the Power and Authority of Almighty God, over life and death. He stayed on earth to teach His disciples, and to commission them to spread the Gospel of Jesus Christ.

Jesus spent time with His disciples preparing them for ministry. He told them to remain in Jerusalem, to await the coming of the Holy Spirit. Acts 1: 8-11 says, "But ye shall receive power, after that the Holy Ghost is come upon you: and ye shall be witnesses unto me both in Jerusalem, and in all Judaea, and in Samaria, and unto the uttermost part of the earth. And when he had spoken these things, while they beheld, he was taken up; and a cloud received him out of their sight. And while they looked steadfastly toward heaven as he went up, behold, two men stood by them in white apparel; Which also said, Ye men of Galilee, why stand ye gazing up into heaven? this same Jesus, which is taken up from you into heaven, shall so come in like manner as ye have seen him go into heaven."

Jesus fulfilled His assignment on earth, to reconcile mankind to God. This is a demonstration of His unhindered love for us. His blood was shed, our atonement secured, and a mission presented to the disciples. Mark 16:19 tells us, "So then after the Lord had spoken unto them, he was received up into heaven, and sat on the right hand of God." Jesus now sits in the holy of holies, at the right hand of Father God. What a journey taken, all on our behalf. Thank you, Jesus!

~Jesus, The Perfect Sacrifice

We are reconciled to God as a result of His perfect sacrifice. His sacrifice enables us to know and experience the love He has for us. Everything in the Bible, from Genesis to Revelation, points to Jesus. There were a few different types of sacrifices, or offerings, that God required of His people under the Old Testament law. We will spend time examining sin offerings, or sin sacrifices. God is Holy, and will have nothing to do with sin. In order for atonement to be made, or forgiveness to be granted, for our sin, a blood sacrifice must be made.

Sin must carry a severe penalty because sin is anything that displeases Almighty God. The Hebrew word for atonement, *Kippur*, means to cover. This is important, because the sacrifice that God commands for sin, covers the sin. God no longer sees it, or counts it against us, if we have placed our faith and trust in Him. These blood sacrifices have been made ever since Adam and Eve sinned in the Garden of Eden.

When Adam and Eve sinned against God, they hid themselves because they were naked. It was not until they sinned, that they even realized that they were naked. God provided them with coverings made of animal hide. An animal had to die, in order to cover them. Their sin resulted in the first animal that was sacrificed to cover, or atone for someone's sin. Genesis 3: 21 tells us, "Unto Adam also and to his wife did the LORD God make coats of skins, and clothed them." God made a blood sacrifice to cover Adam and Eve's sin.

Demonstrated throughout the Old Testament, in accordance with what God required, a blood offering had to be made for the remission of sins. God commanded that a blood sacrifice, of an innocent animal be made, on behalf of sinful man. The requirement of a blood offering, other than our own, places God's mercy on display. Those of us, then and now, who have placed our faith and trust in God, have never had to atone for our own sins. The penalty was taken care of with a blood sacrifice. Time and time again, God has shown mercy, by not giving sinful man what he deserves, which is spiritual death, and separation from God.

The reason the blood sacrifices were offered daily and annually was because the blood of an animal could never permanently atone for sin. It had to continually be performed. Hebrews 10:11-12 tells us, "And every priest standeth daily ministering and offering oftentimes the same sacrifices, which can never take away sins: But this man, after he had offered one sacrifice for sins forever, sat down on the right hand of God." Animal sacrifices were a temporary sin solution, pointing to the future permanent redemptive sacrifice that Christ provides.

Galatians 3:24 says, "So the law was our guardian until Christ came that we might be justified by faith." We see glimpses of Christ throughout the Old Testament. Every time the blood of an innocent lamb was shed as a sin sacrifice to pay the penalty for sin, it foreshadowed Christ's death on the cross. We see Christ in the story of Abraham being told to sacrifice his son, Isaac.

We also see Christ in the book of Exodus chapter twelve, which is referred to as the Passover. This was God's last plague over Egypt, in His attempt to free the Israelites from Egyptian bondage. The Israelites had to put the blood of a lamb over their doorposts. The blood was a sign to pass over those houses. The angel of death came and killed every firstborn Egyptian, but passed over the homes with the blood on the doors. Exodus 12:13 tells us, "And the blood shall be to you for a token upon the houses where ye are: and when I see the blood, I will pass over you, and the plague shall not be upon you to destroy you, when I smite the land of Egypt." This passing over, foreshadows Christ's blood on the cross, protecting those who believe upon His Name.

He had been foreshadowed all throughout history, finally arrived. His name is Jesus. I Corinthians 5:7 says, "For Christ, our Passover lamb, has been sacrificed." We were, and still are, guilty of sin. God's punishment for sin is death, both physically and spiritually. Romans 6:23 says, "For the wages of sin is death; but the gift of God is eternal life through Jesus Christ our Lord." Jesus paid the penalty for all sin.

Jesus is the Passover Lamb. God sent Jesus to do away with the old method of atonement for sin. He became the ultimate, perfect, sinless sacrifice for the sins of all mankind. John the Baptist identified Jesus as such, in John 1:29, where it says, "The next day John saw Jesus coming toward him and said, 'Look, the Lamb of God, who takes away the sin of the world!'" Christ took all of our sin upon himself, on the cross at Calvary.

Jesus literally experienced all sin, in order to bridge the gap between us and Almighty God. It is our sin that separates us from God. Now, if we place our faith and trust in Him, Christ's death on the cross cleanses us of the guilt of our sin.

He paid the price for all those who love Him. Jesus died once, for all the sin of mankind.

John 19:30 tells us, "When Jesus therefore had received the vinegar, he said, It is finished: and he bowed his head, and gave up the ghost." It is finished means that there will never be a need for a sin sacrifice again. His sacrifice for our sin, was perfect, selfless, and sufficient. Through the blood of Jesus, if we place our faith in Him, we are reconciled to God.

Read Isaiah 53.

~Direct Access To God

Having a correct understanding of our access to Almighty God, and our privilege of approaching His throne, is critical. We are unhindered by rituals or rules. We must grasp this truth, in order to walk in freedom with Him. These ideas that God is not personal, that we do not have direct access to Him, or that our prayers can be answered elsewhere, are completely false. The notion that we can receive forgiveness from a priest for our sins against God is completely erroneous. Praying to anyone other than Almighty God, asking anyone but God for forgiveness for our trespasses against Him specifically, or relying on anyone but God for power and authority is futile and ineffective.

There is one God, in the three persons of God the Father, God the Son, and God the Holy Spirit. They, all three, are one. I John 5:7 tells us, "For there are three that bear record in heaven, the Father, the Word, and the Holy Ghost: and these three are one." The death, burial, and resurrection of Jesus Christ, opened up our direct access to God. There had to be a permanent payment for the sin of mankind, in order for us to have a relationship with God. Because of the blood shed by Jesus, we have direct access to God.

There is no one else to whom, or through whom, our prayers and petitions should be given. There is no one else to whom, or through whom, our prayers and petitions will be answered. The Holy Spirit of God lives within all who have placed their faith and trust in Jesus. It is the Holy Spirit who convicts our hearts of sin, and gives us guidance. We can directly approach God anytime, anywhere, and for any reason in Jesus' name. Additionally, God is the only one who can forgive us for our sins against Him. We must have a clear understanding of God, and our privilege of being His children.

God is the only one who we should offer our prayers. He is the only one who can answer our prayers. Praying to anyone, or anything other than God, is an exercise in futility. Some find comfort in praying to Mary, statues, and to "saints"; but these prayers are going nowhere, because there is only one who hears and who is able to answer our prayers, and that is our Heavenly Father, through Jesus Christ. I Timothy 2:5 says, "For there is one God, and one mediator between God and men, the man Christ Jesus." God is holy, and cannot be in the presence of sin. Because of this, He sent Jesus to die for our sins to reconcile us to God. It is through Jesus Christ only, that we have access to God. When we approach God, in Jesus' name, He hears us.

When we sin against God, He is the only one who is capable of forgiving us for our iniquities. Confessing our sins against God to anyone but God will be useless, if God's forgiveness is what we seek. We must not rely on man to do only what God can do. I John 1:9 tells us, "If we confess our sins, he is faithful and just to forgive us our sins, and to cleanse us from all unrighteousness." If we do not repent, and ask forgiveness from God, we will remain unchanged. Forgiveness of sin can only come directly from God.

If you have placed your faith and trust in Jesus, all of your sins are already forgiven. Acts 10:43 says, "To him give all the prophets witness, that through his name whosoever believeth in him shall receive remission of sins." A priest, pastor, elder, or counselor, are all just people with no power to save or forgive trespasses against God and His Word. God is all knowing, all powerful, and able to extend forgiveness, cleanse us of our sin, and clothe us in righteousness.

If prayer or accountability for ourselves, is what we seek, then we can turn to a brother or sister in Christ. James 5:16 says, "Confess your faults one to another, and pray one for another, that ye may be healed. The effectual fervent prayer of a righteous man availeth much." We need to come along side each other, supporting one another through prayer, exhortation, and accountability. I Thessalonians 5:11 tells us, "Wherefore comfort yourselves together, and edify one another, even as also ye do." We are the family of Christ, and this is what Christian community looks like.

If we have offended another, or if we have caused discord among people, we must seek forgiveness from whoever we have offended. Ephesians 4:32 says, "And be ye kind one to another, tenderhearted, forgiving one another, even as God for Christ's sake hath forgiven you." It is necessary to right any wrongs we have with others. To be in right standing and alignment with the will of the Lord, we must have a clear conscience in regard to others. Colossians 3:13 says, "Forbearing one another, and forgiving one another, if any man have a quarrel against any: even as Christ forgave you, so also do ye." God only expects us to do our part, we can't control what others do. We must always be seeking the will of the Lord for our lives.

Let's not ever confuse the roles that people play in our lives, with God's role in our lives. We must appropriately direct our prayers and petitions to God. We must seek prayer and accountability from others. We repent to God for our sin.

We must seek forgiveness from those we have offended or hurt. Finally, we must go before the Lord, repent for our sins, and ask forgiveness. Our God is a personal God, who loves us.

~The Lord Is Our Shepherd

Jehovah-raah; the Lord is my Shepherd. God refers to us as sheep, and He refers to Jesus as our Shepherd, many times throughout the Scriptures. We are called sheep, and we have one Shepherd. In John 10:7-11, Jesus says, "Then said Jesus unto them again, Verily, verily, I say unto you, I am the door of the sheep. All that ever came before me are thieves and robbers: but the sheep did not hear them. I am the door: by me if any man enter in, he shall be saved, and shall go in and out, and find pasture. The thief cometh not, but for to steal, and to kill, and to destroy: I am come that they might have life, and that they might have it more abundantly. I am the good shepherd: the good shepherd giveth his life for the sheep." For everyone who places their hope, faith, and trust in the Lord, they have a faithful shepherd: Jesus. Jesus is The Good Shepherd.

A good shepherd knows all of his sheep. In John 10:14-15, Jesus says, "I am the good shepherd, and know my sheep, and am known of mine. As the Father knoweth me, even so know I the Father: and I lay down my life for the sheep." Jesus knows us by name. He knows everything there is to know about us. Nothing about us, is a mystery to Him. Jesus is The Good Shepherd.

Nothing about us is a surprise to our Lord and Savior, Jesus Christ. He knows us. Psalm 139:1-4 says, "O lord, thou hast searched me, and known me. Thou knowest my downsitting and mine uprising, thou understandest my thought afar off. Thou compassest my path and my lying down, and art acquainted with all my ways. For there is not a word in my tongue, but, lo, O Lord, thou knowest it altogether." Jesus is The Good Shepherd.

He knows our character, our faults, our strengths, our weaknesses, our thoughts, our words before they are spoken, and our actions. Even when we seem to be blending in with the goats, He calls us out by our names. Jesus knows His children, and they know His voice. In John 10:3 Jesus says, "To him the porter openeth; and the sheep hear his voice: and he calleth his own sheep by name, and leadeth them out." Jesus is our shepherd who is omniscient; He knows everything that there is to know about everything, especially us. Jesus is The Good Shepherd.

A good shepherd cares for, protects, and watches over his sheep. Psalm 91:2-4 says, "I will say of the LORD, He is my refuge and my fortress: my God; in him will I trust. Surely, he shall deliver thee from the snare of the fowler, and from the noisome pestilence. He shall cover thee with his feathers, and under his wings shalt thou trust: his truth shall be thy shield and buckler." Psalm 91 is packed full of God's promises of protection and the assurance that no matter what we go through, He will be with us. Jesus is The Good Shepherd.

Psalm 23:1 tells us, "The LORD is my shepherd; I shall not want." Jesus provides all of our needs, so that we lack no good thing. He protects us. Isaiah 54:17 says, "No weapon that is formed against thee shall prosper; and every tongue that shall rise against thee in judgment thou shalt condemn. This is the heritage of the servants of the LORD, and their righteousness is of me, saith the LORD." Jesus is The Good Shepherd.

He guides our steps if we are walking in the Spirit and listening to His voice. Psalm 121:8 says, "The LORD shall preserve thy going out and thy coming in from this time forth, and even for evermore." Jesus is always watching over us, and has our best interests at heart. He is our guardian. He is our watchman; He never leaves His post. Psalm 139:7 says, "Whither shall I go from thy spirit? or whither shall I flee from thy presence?" Jesus is The Good Shepherd.

A good shepherd will go after lost sheep, even just one. Jesus will pursue those who are lost. He does not want any to spend eternity apart from Him. He continues to pursue those who trust in Him, as well. He will never stop pursuing our hearts and minds. In Luke 15:4, Jesus says, "What man of you, having a hundred sheep, if he loses one of them, doth not leave the ninety and nine in the wilderness, and go after that which is lost, until he finds it?" We are not just numbers to God; He will go after those who go astray, or who are lost. We matter to God. Jesus is The Good Shepherd.

He longs for us to abide in Him. 1 Peter 2:25 says, "For ye were as sheep going astray; but are now returned unto the Shepherd and Bishop of your souls." The Lord desires that we stay in His fold. Jesus is The Good Shepherd.

A good shepherd will lay down his life to save his sheep. This is precisely what Jesus did for us. He paid the price for our sin, with His life. How could we do anything but accept what He did for us, and believe. John 10:11 tells us, "I am the good shepherd: the good shepherd giveth his life for the sheep." Jesus died so that we could live. We do not deserve the grace and mercy that Christ provides us, but He pours it out anyway. Romans 5:8 says, "But God commendeth his love toward us, in that, while we were yet sinners, Christ died for us."

Sin separates us from Almighty God, but through Christ's death, we are reconciled to God. He made a way for us, by laying His life down. Because of Christ's sacrifice, we can spend eternity with God. Romans 6:23 tells us, "For the wages of sin is death; but the gift of God is eternal life through Jesus Christ our Lord." Jesus is The Good Shepherd.

Thank you, Jesus, for being our one, and only, Shepherd. Without Jesus shepherding us, we would go astray, and be lost for all eternity. He made the ultimate sacrifice for His sheep, so that we could spend eternity with Him. Romans 4:25 says, "Who was delivered for our offences, and was raised again for our justification." Thanks be to God, for loving us, and rescuing all who call upon His name. 1 Peter 3:18 tells us, "For Christ also hath once suffered for sins, the just for the unjust, that he might bring us to God, being put to death in the flesh, but quickened by the Spirit:" Jesus is The Good Shepherd.

~Jesus Is

It is very clear in Scripture that Jesus is Truth. He is life everlasting, and a direct connection to God the Father. We must have a proper understanding about who Jesus is. In John 14:6 Jesus says, "I am the way, the truth, and the life: no man cometh unto the Father, but by me." Jesus is The Way. Jesus is The Truth. Jesus is The Life.

Let's examine this life changing declaration, that Jesus made about Himself. Our belief in and understanding of John 14:6 is critical to our salvation. Jesus is the Savior of our souls. He puts purpose and meaning into our lives. When we place our faith in Him, we truly place it in The Way, The Truth, and The Life.

"I am the way:"

Jesus Christ, God's only son, born of a virgin, came to earth as a human. He entered our space as a baby, and grew into adulthood among us. He lived on earth as a human for over thirty years. He died on the cross as payment for all the sin of humanity past, present, and future. As promised, He rose on the third day, and is now seated at the right hand of God. He did all of this to be the way for our sins to be forgiven, and for mankind to be reconciled to God. Jesus is the way.

Jesus is not a way, but the only Way. There are not some, a few, or many ways to God, everlasting life, freedom, and heaven. There is one Way to access all these things, and Jesus is the Way.

Jesus is the only way to life everlasting. Romans 6:23 says, "For the wages of sin is death; but the gift of God is eternal life through Jesus Christ our LORD." Placing your faith in Jesus is the only way to experience eternal life spent in the presence of the Lord. John 3:16 assures us, "For God so loved the world, that he gave his only begotten Son, that whosoever believeth in him should not perish, but have everlasting life." There is no other way, but Jesus.

Jesus is the only way to freedom. Galatians 5:1 says, "Stand fast therefore in the liberty wherewith Christ hath made us free, and be not entangled again with the yoke of bondage." Jesus is the only way to freedom from sin and shame. II Corinthians 3:17 tells us, "Now the LORD is that Spirit: and where the Spirit of the LORD is, there is liberty." He frees us from the penalty of sin. Where the spirit of the Lord is, there is freedom.

Jesus is our gateway to heaven. There is no other way, but by faith in Jesus, to go to heaven. In John 14:2 Jesus says, "In my Father's house are many mansions: if it were not so, I would have told you. I go to prepare a place for you." Jesus is the way.

"I am the Truth:"

John 1:14 says, "And the Word was made flesh, and dwelt among us, (and we beheld his glory, the glory as of the only begotten of the Father,) full of grace and truth." God's Word is Truth. Jesus is the manifestation of God's Word. Jesus came in the flesh as God's Word. He is Truth. Truth cannot be found anywhere else.

Jesus is the embodiment of all truth from Genesis to Revelation. Everything within the pages of The Word of God, points directly to Him. John 17:17 says, "Sanctify them through thy truth: thy word is truth." We can trust the Word of God, which has been tested and tried for centuries. It is the infallible Word of God. Jesus is the infallible Word of God in the flesh. Jesus is Truth.

Truth cannot be found anywhere else but in Jesus. He is Truth; in Him there is no deception or lie. John 8:31-32 tells us, "Then said Jesus to those Jews which believed on Him, If ye continue in my word, then are ye my disciples indeed; And ye shall know the truth, and the truth shall make you free." Jesus is Truth.

"I am the Life:"

Jesus laid down His life so that we could live. The death of Jesus, provides us with freedom from sin and death. In John 8:24, Jesus says, "I said therefore unto you, that ye shall die in your sins: for if ye believe not that I am he, ye shall die in your sins." His death, burial, and resurrection provide us with the opportunity to truly live. He is the Life.

There is no life apart from Jesus Christ. John 8:12 says, "Then spake Jesus again unto them, saying, I am the light of the world: he that followeth me shall not walk in darkness, but shall have the light of life." Christ did it all for us. By accepting what He did on the cross for us, we can have eternal life with Him.

He paid the penalty for our sin one time, for all. Christ laid down His life so that through Him, we might live. In John 11:25-26, Jesus said to Martha, "I am the resurrection, and the life: he that believeth in me, though he were dead, yet shall he live: And whosoever liveth and believeth in me shall never die. Believest thou this?" If we truly believe, we will live, because He lives within us. Jesus is Life.

"No man comes to the Father but by me:"

It is only through a relationship with Christ that we have access to God. Jesus is the only pathway to God. I Timothy 2:5 says, "For there is one God, and one mediator between God and men, the man Christ Jesus." We cannot have fellowship with God without Jesus. Jesus was the final atonement for our sin, that bridged the gap between us and God. We now have direct access.

Jesus is our link, so to speak. Placing our faith and trust in Christ, and asking Him into our lives, gives us direct access to the King of Kings. Jesus is the only way we have access to Almighty God. Jesus is truly all we need.

Let's, by faith, believe and unlock our access to our Heavenly Father.

~God Draws Men To Himself

God, through the work of His Holy Spirit, draws us to Himself. The Holy Spirit of God relentlessly pursues our hearts, and draws us to Himself.

God draws those who are far from Him, to Himself. He does this through the Holy Spirit's pursuit of our hearts. It is a beautiful pursuit that never ceases. He continually draws us into fellowship with Him. God's pursuit of our hearts is relentless. John 6:44-45 tells us, "No man can come to me, except the Father which hath sent me draw him: and I will raise him up at the last day." It is not by chance or coincidence, that we come into relationship with Jesus. God draws us to Himself.

God has given us free will to choose life through a relationship with Him, or death and eternal separation from Him. Either way, it is ultimately our choice. His desire is for us to experience life's journey in an intimate relationship with Him. He never gives up the pursuit of our hearts. As long as we live, He will pursue us, as He draws us to Himself. It does not end when we surrender the reigns of our lives over to Him. The Holy Spirit of God continues to pursue us, in order for us to experience spiritual growth. The Holy Spirit continuously draws us into a deeper and more meaningful relationship with Him.

You may ask, "Who is this Holy Spirit"? Following his life on earth, His death, His burial, and His resurrection, Jesus ascended into heaven. In His physical absence, He sent His Holy Spirit to be with us. The Holy Spirit of God convicts our hearts of sin. The Holy Spirit dwells in us. The Holy Spirit is our counselor, guide, and help at all times.

God the Father, God the Son, and God the Holy Spirit, are all one, but each with different attributes. The Holy Spirit of God is our comforter, counselor, and guide. It is the Holy Spirit who pursues our hearts and minds. It is the Holy Spirit who compels our hearts and minds to believe. That tug, that nudge, that conviction that changes our hearts, is the Holy Spirit of God. We must not ignore the Spirit of our living God, who is actively pursuing us.

Isaiah 53:6 tells us, "All we like sheep have gone astray; we have turned everyone to his own way; and the Lord hath laid on him the iniquity of us all." We naturally go our own way. We naturally "sin," or go astray from God. I Peter 2:25 also says, "For ye were as sheep going astray; but are now returned unto the Shepherd and Bishop of your souls." No matter how hard or fast we run from the Lord, God still continues to draw us to Himself. He will not give up on us.

God sent His son, Jesus, to the cross as payment for our sins. Because of this great gift, we have access to our Father in heaven. Our sin separates us from God. Jesus' blood covers our sin debt. It is because of the blood of Jesus that we do not have to earn our right standing with God. The only requirement is that we surrender our lives to the Lord God Almighty.

The Holy Spirit draws us to God, even in our sinful condition. Ephesians 1:18 says, "The eyes of your understanding being enlightened; that ye may know what is the hope of his calling, and what the riches of the glory of his inheritance in the saints." The Holy Spirit of God opens the eyes of our hearts and minds to understand the call God has on our lives. No matter what we have done, or where we have been, we are still welcomed by God. He loves us, and desires to change our hearts. No matter what condition we are in, we can still choose Christ.

John 6:65 says, "And he said, therefore said I unto you, that no man can come unto me, except it were given unto him of my Father." God draws us to Himself. He is waiting to break every chain that keeps us bound to our sin. Romans 1:16 further clarifies the drawing of The Holy Spirit of God when it says, "For I am not ashamed of the gospel of Christ: for it is the power of God unto salvation to everyone that believes." The Holy Spirit of God draws us to Himself, but we have to choose Him.

God's invitation to dwell in His presence is always open to us. He never withdraws the call. We choose Him freely, therefore, we will have authenticity in our walk with Christ. His drawing, and His pursuit are always gentle. It is our decision whether we accept or reject God's gift of eternal life. God's ultimate desire for us, is the salvation of our souls.

Walking in victory over sin and death: this is true freedom!

Respond with a surrendered heart to the drawing of the Holy Spirit of God.

~God's Unparalleled Love For Us

There is no love that even compares to the love that God has for us. To experience His great love is to truly live. Ephesians 3:18-19 says, "That ye… May be able to comprehend with all saints what is the breadth, and length, and depth, and height; And to know the love of Christ, which passeth knowledge, that ye might be filled with all the fullness of God." God's love for us is pure, eternal, and unmatched.

We often hear people casually say to one another, "God loves you." How often do we really stop to think about the truly amazing love He has for us? We tend to take for granted the power and strength of God's love. There is no earthly being who is capable of loving us the way that God does. The Almighty, all powerful, all knowing God loves us unconditionally.

Although we turn our backs and run from Him, He still loves us. He knows everything there is to know about us, and in His perfection, He still loves us. We sin, but He tells us that Christ's blood was shed to pay the penalty for our sin. He loves us. He is holy, and we are not. He still loves us. God's love is unrivaled, unthinkable, unwavering, sacrificial, powerful, perfect, and relentless. He is God, and He loves us.

His love for us is sacrificial. Our sin separates us from Holy God. In order for us to approach God, He sent His only begotten, sinless Son to earth. Jesus came to earth to die for the atonement of our sins. He did this for us, to reconcile mankind to Himself. He did this out of His immeasurable love for us. Just marinate in the perfect love of God.

John 3:16 says, "For God so loved the world, that he gave his only begotten Son, that whosoever believeth in him should not perish, but have everlasting life." We did nothing to deserve this sacrificial manifestation of His love. His enduring love for us initiated this sacrificial act on our behalf. No one loves us like Almighty God.

He gives us the opportunity to choose everlasting life, through our belief, faith, and trust in Jesus. I John 4:10 says, "Herein is love, not that we loved God, but that he loved us, and sent his Son to be the propitiation for our sins." If we stop and marvel at His love on display through this selfless act, how could we not be persuaded to love Him in return. His love draws us into His presence, and compels us to stay.

His love precedes us. God had us on His heart, before the foundation of the world. Ephesians 1:4 says, "According as he hath chosen us in him before the foundation of the world, that we should be holy and without blame before him in love." His desire has always been our holiness, and right standing with Him. He loved each of us before we took our first breaths. God chose us for Himself before He created us. He has always loved us.

God's love for us is evident in how he carefully creates us. He cradles us in our mother's womb. He meticulously fashions every detail of our being. We are His workmanship, and He loves us.

Psalm 139:13-16 says, "For thou hast possessed my reins: thou hast covered me in my mother's womb. I will praise thee; for I am fearfully and wonderfully made: marvelous are thy works; and that my soul knoweth right well. My substance was not hid from thee, when I was made in secret, and curiously wrought in the lowest parts of the earth. Thine eyes did see my substance, yet being imperfect; and in thy book all my members were written, which in continuance were fashioned, when as yet there was none of them." He has been passionately caring for us, loving us, and pursuing us, since before we were even born.

His love for us is enduring. God's love for us is without end. Psalm 136:1 says, "Give thanks to the Lord, for he is good, for his steadfast love endures forever (ESV)." His love endures, even if we do not reciprocate. He is patient, and He does not grow weary as He waits. We have to, by an act of our free will, accept His calling on our lives to spend forever in His presence. He still loves us, regardless of our choice. Romans 5:8 tells us, "But God commendeth his love toward us, in that, while we were yet sinners, Christ died for us."

Where we spend eternity is ultimately our choice, and contingent on our acceptance or rejection of Jesus. On the other hand, His love for us is not contingent. His love endures. Holy God continues to love us, even if we reject His love. Our rejection of His love results in eternal consequences, which is eternal separation from Him. He still loves us, even when we choose to be separated from Him for all eternity. His perpetual love for us is one of a kind. This type of love can only be given by the Lord.

His love for us is relentless. Romans 8:38-39 "For I am persuaded, that neither death, nor life, nor angels, nor principalities, nor powers, nor things present, nor things to come, Nor height, nor depth, nor any other creature, shall be able to separate us from the love of God, which is in Christ Jesus our Lord." God never gives up on us. He is in continual pursuit of our hearts and minds. He makes every effort to turn our hearts toward Him. His love is relentless.

His love for us is patient. Our Lord and Savior, Jesus Christ, has been patient with us since the creation of mankind. He does not immediately give us what we deserve for our sin. His mercy endures, and He gives us time to surrender. When He returns for us, His bride, our time to choose Him will end. Lamentations 3: 22-23 says, "It is of the Lord's mercies that we are not consumed, because his compassions fail not. They are new every morning: great is thy faithfulness." He patiently waits for us to repent and surrender our lives to Him before His final judgement.

His wrath will come; but in the meantime, He patiently waits for our repentance. The perfect patience of Christ, was beautifully displayed in Paul's life. In I Timothy 1:16, Paul says, "Howbeit for this cause I obtained mercy, that in me first Jesus Christ might shew forth all longsuffering, for a pattern to them which should hereafter believe on him to life everlasting." Paul persecuted Christ followers, but the Lord was patient with Paul. Paul had an encounter with the Lord that changed the course of his life. He desires to have a life changing encounter with everyone.

He is patient with us. II Peter 3:9 says, "The Lord is not slack concerning his promise, as some men count slackness; but is longsuffering to us-ward, not willing that any should perish, but that all should come to repentance." His patience has no flaws, but it will not last forever. God's patience will cease at the final judgement when He returns. Through the Holy Spirit, God draws man to Himself. While we still have the option, let us respond with a resounding, "Yes, Lord, Yes!"

The love God has for us is beyond our ability to fully comprehend. His love for us is untainted, it is perfect. He continues to love us, even if we do not love Him in return. He loves us with all of our quirks, idiosyncrasies, flaws, bad habits, moods, etc. He loves us so much that He sent His only Son as payment for our sins. He loves us so much that upon receiving Christ back at His side, He sent us His Holy Spirit to dwell within us. He loves us so much that He tarries His return. He is giving us ample time to turn our hearts to Him.

His love has no bounds. His love has no comparison. He is God Almighty, the lover of our souls.

~Abba Father

We have the incredible privilege of referring to Almighty God, as *Abba Father*. Abba Father, is only used three times in the Bible. Paul refers to God in this way twice, and Jesus calls God Abba Father in the Garden of Gethsemane, shortly before He was crucified. Both Paul and Jesus had uniquely intimate, and dramatically life changing, relationships with God. Abba Father is our God.

Galatians 4:6 says, "And because ye are sons, God hath sent forth the Spirit of his Son into your hearts, crying, Abba, Father." Abba means Father in the Aramaic. It is an affectionate and endearing term used by children for their Daddy. When we place our faith and trust in Christ, the Holy Spirit of God now resides in us, and we are immediately adopted into the family of God.

Just like Paul and Jesus, we are intimately connected to God. God knows us better than anyone, including ourselves. He is more intimately acquainted with us than anyone. We are God's children. Just as earthly fathers are called Daddy by their children, we can humbly call Almighty God, Abba Father as well. In Mark 14:36 Jesus says, "And he said, Abba, Father, all things are possible unto thee; take away this cup from me: nevertheless, not what I will, but what thou wilt."

Jesus is God's only begotten Son. Jesus came to earth, as a man, to die for the sins of mankind. Jesus calls God Abba Father, because of their tender, affectionate relationship. Their bond demonstrates the kind of love that is pure and undefiled.

Jesus knew that God can do all things, and He is in control of all things. He cried out Abba Father, not my will but yours be done. He places ultimate trust in His Father, God.

The intensity of love that exists between God the Father, and God the Son, is indescribable. Because we are God's children, this intimacy is offered to us by God the Father, as well. We are able to approach God, through the blood of Jesus, in this same intimate way. We, as sons and daughters of the King of Kings, have the same level of intimacy afforded to us. We have the privilege of addressing God as Abba Father. God loves us so much that He gave Jesus as payment for our sin. John 3:16 tells us, "For God so loved the world, that he gave his only begotten Son, that whosoever believeth in him should not perish, but have everlasting life."

His desire has always been to be in relationship with us. His love for us was evident before our conception. We are adopted into the family of God, which means we are chosen. When you are adopted, you are handpicked and dearly loved. Knowing our flaws and our shortcomings, He still chooses us. He loves us deeply. We show our gratitude and deep love, by praising Him as Abba Father.

In Romans 8:14-17, Paul identifies and describes our adoption process. "For as many as are led by the Spirit of God, they are the sons of God. For ye have not received the spirit of bondage again to fear; but ye have received the Spirit of adoption, whereby we cry, Abba Father. The Spirit itself beareth witness with our spirit, that we are the children of God: And if children, then heirs; heirs of God, and joint-heirs with Christ; if so be that we suffer with him, that we may be also glorified together."

We are children of God, through the work of the Holy Spirit, adopting us into the family of God. We are grafted into the family, fully united as His children. We approach our Father with warmth and intimacy. We call Him Daddy, or Abba Father. We are given the same permission and honor to experience the level of familiarity and attachment as natural sons and daughters. We now share in the inheritance of Jesus Christ. What belongs to Christ, also belongs to us. God is called by many names. Abba Father demonstrates intense intimacy that is shared between a loving daddy and his children. What an honor it is to be called the children of God.

~John 3:16

John 3:16 is a very powerful promise in Scripture. It is the cornerstone of the majority of my writing. You will see that I refer to it often.

In one verse, John 3:16 sums up the main theme expressed throughout the entire Bible, from Genesis through Revelation. This verse provides the hope and promise that all of humankind needs. John 3:16 brings hope to the hopeless, love to the unlovable, faith to the faithless, security to the insecure, worth to the worthless, righteousness to the unrighteous, and life to the lifeless. This is a summation of the Gospel of Jesus Christ, in one short and simple verse.

> "For God so loved the world, that he gave his
> only begotten Son, that whosoever believeth in
> him should not perish, but have everlasting life."

"For God:"

Make no mistake, there is only one true God. Isaiah 45:5 says, "I am the Lord, and there is none else, there is no God beside me: I girded thee, though thou hast not known me:" God presents Himself in three persons who are all divinely God: God the Father, God the Son, and God the Holy Spirit. In

John 10:30, Jesus says, "I and my Father are one." Jesus is referred to as "The Word," in the Bible. John 1:14 tells us, "And the Word was made flesh, and dwelt among us, (and we beheld his glory, the glory as of the only begotten of the Father,) full of grace and truth."

So, Almighty God, Creator of the world, and everything in it, is three in One. He is The One. I John 5:7 says, "For there are three that bear record in heaven, the Father, the Word, and the Holy Ghost: and these three are one." God is, and was, and forever will be. He is.

"So loved the world:"

God created the world, and He created us. We are His design, and His love for us is perfect. Only Holy God is capable of pure, unconditional love. His love for us never ends, even if we choose not to receive it. He does not demand that we reciprocate His love, but not doing so will result in eternal separation from God. I John 4:10 tells us, "Herein is love, not that we loved God, but that he loved us, and sent his Son to be the propitiation for our sins." God's love for us is unmatched, relentless, and unmovable.

"He gave His only begotten Son:"

God's love for us is demonstrative. Romans 5:8 says, "But God commendeth his love toward us, in that, while we were yet sinners, Christ died for us." God knew that we were incapable of keeping the Old Testament law, and that we would fail to perform the sacrifices that needed to be made continually in order to atone for the sins of mankind. This was God's law. We needed to be held accountable for our sin. It all pointed to the coming of Jesus.

God required a perfect, sinless sacrifice, who He would provide. Jesus stepped down from His heavenly throne, became human, lived, was crucified, bore our sin, rose from the grave, and ascended back to His rightful place in heaven. Jesus took on all of the sin of the world: past, present, and future. He did this to reconcile us to God. No further sacrifice was, or will ever be needed. God loves us this much.

"that whosoever believeth in him should not perish:"

It is by faith that we believe. "Whosoever" indicates that anyone can spend eternity in the presence of our Lord, if only he believes. It is a matter of surrendering our will for the will of Father God. To perish, is to die. To die, is to face damnation. Through our belief, and through placing our faith and trust in Almighty God, we will not perish, but we will live. II Peter 3:9 says, "The Lord is not slack concerning his promise, as some men count slackness; but is longsuffering to us-ward, not willing that any should perish, but that all should come to repentance." We must allow The Holy Spirit of God to exchange our unbelief for belief.

"but have everlasting life:"

The ultimate prize, and the ultimate result of placing our faith, and trust in the Lord, is everlasting, eternal life. John 3:36 tells us, "He that believeth on the Son hath everlasting life: and he that believeth not the Son shall not see life; but the wrath of God abideth on him." There is nothing sweeter than this promise.

When we place our faith and trust in Jesus, who shed His blood to reconcile us to God, we are assured eternal, everlasting life in His presence. John 10:28 says, "And I give unto them eternal life; and they shall never perish, neither shall any man pluck them out of my hand." We must allow the Holy Spirit of God to exchange the penalty for our sin, which is death and separation, for life everlasting through faith in Jesus Christ.

John 3:16 says, "For God so loved the world, that he gave his only begotten Son, that whosoever believeth in him should not perish, but have everlasting life." God adores us, He sent Jesus to be the payment for our sin. He did it all so that our sin would no longer be a barrier between us. The work has been done, and now the choice to accept God's gift of eternal life is ours. We are loved by God.

~Our Response To The Love Of God

God, The Almighty One, is worthy of our love.

Sometimes we need to reflect on our relationship with God, and what it looks like to love Him. Specifically, we need to marvel at the reasons we love Him. Love is a choice. How we express our love toward God is a direct response to how we understand, and experience the love God has for us. We must examine why we have chosen to love God. We must refrain from simply saying we love God, without knowing why.

We love Him because He has commanded it. In Exodus 20:3 God says, "Thou shalt have no other gods before me." In Mark 12:30 we read, "And thou shalt love the Lord thy God with all thy heart, and with all thy soul, and with all thy mind, and with all thy strength: this is the first commandment." God created us to love Him. Yes, God has commanded us to love Him, but we have to choose to do so.

We love Him because He first loved us, and we find it impossible to resist the love God lavishes on us. I John 4:19 reads, "We love Him, because He first loved us." He loved us, even when we didn't acknowledge Him at all. Psalm 139:16 tells us, "Thine eyes did see my substance, yet being imperfect; and in thy book all my members were written, which in continuance were fashioned, when as yet there was none of them." When we come to realize that God knew us and loved us before we took our first breaths, how could we do anything but love Him?

We love Him because He is faithful, and He draws us out of darkness into the light. He draws us to Himself. In Jeremiah 31: 3, he is speaking of Israel, but it applies to all generations, including us: "The Lord hath appeared of old unto me, saying, Yea, I have loved thee with an everlasting love: therefore with loving kindness have I drawn thee."

We love Him for rescuing us from darkness. I Peter 2:9 says, " But ye are a chosen generation, a royal priesthood, an holy nation, a peculiar people; that ye should shew forth the praises of him who hath called you out of darkness into his marvellous light;" God has called us to Himself, and we no longer are hidden in the darkness of sin and shame. God draws us to Himself.

We love Him because He gave His only son, Jesus, to die for our sins. Romans 5:8 says, "But God commendeth his love toward us, in that, while we were yet sinners, Christ died for us." When we consider the amazing sacrifice that God made out of His love for us, so that we could be reconciled to Him, our hearts should well up with gratitude and love. I John 4:10 tells us, "Herein is love, not that we loved God, but that he loved us, and sent his Son to be the propitiation for our sins." God's love is so great for us, that He gave His one and only Son to bridge the gap between us.

We love Him because He forgives us of our sins. He gives us a clean slate when we place our trust in Him. He no longer remembers our sin. I John 1:9 tells us, " If we confess our sins, He is faithful and just to forgive us our sins, and to cleanse us of all unrighteousness." With forgiveness comes freedom. To experience forgiveness from God is to experience life in a new and refreshing way.

Consider the many more specific reasons that you love
God. Call to remembrance all that He has done for you. Think
about all He has seen you through. Think about His majesty,
and stand in awe of His greatness. He is an awesome God,
and worthy of our love.

~ God's Grace

God's grace sustains us. His grace strengthens and encourages us. This unmerited favor that God extends to us is a gift from Him. Ephesians 2:8-9 tells us, "For by grace are ye saved through faith; and that not of yourselves: it is the gift of God: Not of works, lest any man should boast." It is because of grace, that we can have a personal relationship with our Lord and Savior, Jesus Christ. Titus 2:11 says, "For the grace of God that bringeth salvation hath appeared to all men," There is nothing that we must do to earn grace, but His grace will change us.

It is our flawed impression of God that keeps us far from Him. Instead of believing that God extends grace to us, we tend to believe that God is a harsh, demanding, and punitive God. We associate God and Christianity with a list of rules that must be followed, and a life void of enjoyment and adventure. Until we come to a proper understanding of God's love, our hearts stay distant with disbelief. It is only when God draws us to Himself, and reveals His true character to us, that our hearts begin to soften. God's Grace changes us.

Coming to a proper understanding of God's love for us is a huge step for most people. We typically know nothing about the grace of God. When He illuminates the truth of His Word for us, and opens the eyes of our hearts and minds to receive the message of God's grace, our heart's posture toward God begins to change. His grace is not freedom to keep sinning, but an invitation to be free from sin. God's Grace changes us.

God's grace is manifested on the cross where Jesus died for the sins of all mankind. Romans 3:23-24 says, "For all have sinned, and come short of the glory of God; Being justified freely by his grace through the redemption that is in Christ Jesus." We did nothing to deserve this favor from Almighty God, who gave His only son to die in our place for our sins. Because of God's grace, our sins and the consequences of our sins were nailed to the cross of Christ.

His grace, through Christ's death, opens the opportunity for us to be reconciled to God through Christ. II Corinthians 5:18 says, "And all things are of God, who hath reconciled us to himself by Jesus Christ, and hath given to us the ministry of reconciliation." God's grace changes us.

God's grace is tremendous. It is only because of Christ's blood, which was shed on the cross, that we are able to experience this favor bestowed upon us through Jesus. For Christians, walking in the light of God's grace brings freedom. We embrace the fact that God's grace is likened to receiving all the benefits of someone that labors diligently to earn favor from the one whom they serve. The difference is that we get the favor, without performing the labor. Romans 11:6 tells us, "And if by grace, then is it no more of works: otherwise grace is no more grace. But if it be of works, then is it no more grace: otherwise work is no more work." God's grace changes us.

II Corinthians 12:9 says, "And he said unto me, My grace is sufficient for thee: for my strength is made perfect in weakness. Most gladly therefore will I rather glory in my infirmities, that the power of Christ may rest upon me." Because of God's grace, He draws us to Himself.

We can come to Christ, and be saved, without having strings attached. God wants our hearts, and He showers us with favor that we do not deserve, in order to draw us into right relationship with Him. II Corinthians 5:17 assures us, "Therefore if any man be in Christ, he is a new creature: old things are passed away; behold, all things are become new." God's grace changes us.

Bask in the radiance of His grace, and be forever thankful that Christ paid the price for our sin. God's grace is sufficient. God's grace changes us.

~God's Mercy

God's mercy extended to us, is an awesome display of His character and who He is. The penalty for our sin requires the punishment of death and eternal separation from God. But God, as a result of His mercy, has not imposed upon us what we deserve, if we place our faith and trust in Him.

We live in a culture that demands that people get what they deserve as a result of their bad choices. Every day the media portrays the outcry of the need for justice to be served on perpetrators of various crimes. Even on a smaller scale, in social and community circles, we tend to forget about the importance of showing mercy to others.

Our society has been conditioned, of late, to not exemplify hearts of mercy and compassion to the least and worst of offenders, if or when they repent and follow Jesus. Yes, consequences need to be in place for criminals, but we need to always remember the mercy that was, currently is, and will be extended to those who place their faith and trust in Jesus. Often times, we fail to recall the mercy that has been poured out to us sinners when we surrender our lives to Christ's authority and Lordship.

The greatest demonstration of mercy was displayed on the Cross at Calvary. John 3:16 "For God so loved the world, that he gave his only begotten Son, that whosoever believeth in him should not perish, but have everlasting life." This is the perfect model of mercy being extended to those who are otherwise undeserving. What we deserve, as sinners, is God's wrath and eternal separation from Him. Yes, this will happen if there is no repentance and surrender to God. On the other hand, He showers us with mercy, if we place our faith and trust in Jesus.

The result of our belief is everlasting life spent with the Lord. Ephesians 2:4-5 says, "But God, who is rich in mercy, for his great love wherewith he loved us, even when we were dead in sins, hath quickened us together with Christ, (by grace ye are saved;)." The punishment for our sin should be the eternal wrath of God. Our sin created spiritual death, but upon our profession of faith in Jesus, God quickens us, and we are alive in Christ. He does not give us what we deserve. Instead, His mercy abounds on our behalf. Thankfully, God is rich in mercy.

In Psalm 51:1-2, David cries out to God for mercy when he says, "Have mercy upon me, O God, according to thy lovingkindness: according unto the multitude of thy tender mercies blot out my transgressions. Wash me thoroughly from mine iniquity, and cleanse me from my sin." Although David did some incredibly bad things (adultery, murder, pride, etc.), David was considered by God to be a man after God's own heart.

The reason is in Acts 13:22. It says, "And when he had removed him, he raised up unto them David to be their king; to whom also he gave testimony, and said, I have found David the son of Jesse, a man after mine own heart, which shall fulfil all my will." David gained favor from God, because he did what God wanted him to do, and he sought after God. He repented of his sins, and was shown mercy.

We serve a God who shows an abundance of mercy. Micah 7:18 says, "Who is a God like unto thee, that pardoneth iniquity, and passeth by the transgression of the remnant of his heritage? He retaineth not his anger forever, because he delighteth in mercy." We can do nothing in and of ourselves to earn God's mercy. His mercy covers the sin of all who seek Him, and place their faith and trust in Him alone.

It is God's delight to show mercy to those who turn from their sin, and surrender their lives to the Lord. Isaiah 55:7 says, "Let the wicked forsake his way, and the unrighteous man his thoughts: and let him return unto the Lord, and he will have mercy upon him; and to our God, for he will abundantly pardon."

We receive a pardon/pass for our sin when we trust in the Lord. God erases the penalty that was purposed for our sins. God's mercy covers us, the moment we place our trust in Him. Hebrews 8:12 assures us, "For I will be merciful to their unrighteousness, and their sins and their iniquities will I remember no more." This is extremely liberating. We receive a clean slate when we come to faith in Jesus.

God's mercy extended to us, when we place our faith and trust in Jesus, should compel us to continue to faithfully walk in the righteousness that Jesus' blood clothed us in.

~Lord, Your Name Is A Strong Tower

The name of the Lord is a Strong Tower. Proverbs 18:10 tells us, "The name of the LORD is a strong tower: the righteous runneth into it, and is safe. The rich man's wealth is his strong city, and as a high wall in his own conceit."

The name of the Lord is a Strong Tower, and those who place their faith and trust in Him have security and safety. In the midst of all the chaos and turmoil in the world, we can take refuge in the Lord. Although we are surrounded by evil, oppression, and unrest, we do not have to be shaken. The name of the Lord is a Strong Tower; He cannot be moved.

He knows the future, and we can be sure that our feet are on solid ground if we trust in the Lord, our Strong Tower. The walls of our Strong Tower are secure, impenetrable, and indestructible. Our Strong Tower isn't going anywhere. Our Lord is a Strong Tower, and He is eternal. He is Almighty God, Lord of Lords.

Proverbs 18: 11 says, "The rich man's wealth is his strong city, and as a high wall in his own conceit." This verse shows a contrast between those who place their faith and trust in God the Strong Tower, and those who place their faith and trust in riches. Wealth as a strong city is not secure. There is no dependability in wealth. Wealth fluctuates, and can vanish with little or no warning. There is no eternal value in wealth.

We cannot take wealth with us when we die. We cannot take shelter in wealth. Wealth does not offer us authentic peace, nor does it give us refuge in the storms of life. Wealth is temporary, whereas The Lord, our Strong Tower, is eternal.

The Lord is a Strong Tower. There are many names of the Lord that describe His attributes. These attributes further portray the Lord as a Strong Tower. When we know some of the names of the Lord that are used throughout the Bible, we can see why He is a Strong Tower for us.

There is no other name greater, or more powerful than the Lord. He is a Strong Tower. Run into it with a humble heart. Run into it with faith. Run into it believing. Run into it with trust. Run into it with a repentant heart. El Shaddai is God Almighty. Psalm 91:1 says it all, "He that dwelleth in the secret place of the most High shall abide under the shadow of the Almighty."

Alpha and Omega is the beginning and the end. Revelation 1:8 says, "I am Alpha and Omega, the beginning and the ending, saith the Lord, which is, and which was, and which is to come, the Almighty." El Roi is the God who sees. Genesis 16:13 tells us, "And she called the name of the Lord that spake unto her, Thou God seest me: for she said, Have I also here looked after him that seeth me?" El Elyon is God Most High. Psalm 92:8 says, "But thou, Lord, art most high for evermore" Yahweh is The Lord, I AM. There are many more names of the Lord that show that He is our Strong Tower. Take some time, and look them up yourself.

We can see why He is reliable, with unmatched strength and power. We can see why we can trust Him for safety and security. We can rest assured that He is our refuge, and our shelter. We can rest assured that nothing can hinder or destroy God, our Strong Tower. The name of the Lord is a Strong Tower that will not move, will not change, will not be hidden, and will not be defeated. Psalm 61:3 says, "For thou hast been a shelter for me, and a strong tower from the enemy." We are protected and secure within the power of His name.

~Jehovah Nissi: The Lord is My Banner

Praise Jesus, The Lord is our Banner. I think of Jehovah Nissi as fighting our battles. He is the One who goes before us, as a covering, and as a declaration of who we are, and who we belong to. In Exodus Chapter 17, Moses was growing weary of the complaints of the Israelites. Moses cried out to the Lord for help. God tells Moses to smite a rock, with the same rod he smote the river, and water will come out, because the Israelites were thirsty. The Lord is our Banner.

Joshua, with the Israelite men, fought Amalek. Every time Moses held up the rod of God in his hand, Israel prevailed. If he let it down Amalek prevailed. When he grew tired, Aaron and Hur held Moses' hands up all night. Moses built an alter, and called it "Jehovah Nissi," The Lord my Banner.

The Lord was their Banner in battle, when they were not fighting with, or relying on their own strength. The Lord is our Banner in battle, as well, when we do not attempt to fight in our own strength. All of our battles belong to The Lord. Exodus 15:3 says, "The Lord is a man of war: The Lord is his name." When we are walking in His light, He will fight our battles.

Our Banner, the Lord, is always victorious, and He fights for us. Ephesians 6:12 tells us, "For we wrestle not against flesh and blood, but against principalities, against powers, against the rulers of the darkness of this world, against spiritual wickedness in high places." We do not have what it takes, within ourselves, to come against this type of enemy. The Lord my Banner, has more than what it takes. We need to allow God, our Banner, to fight our battles.

Just like Moses and the Israelites, if we trust God, and believe that He is big enough to fight our battles, He will. When we try to fight life's battles (of which there are many) on our own, it is far more challenging. When we allow God, in His strength, to fight for us, whether we see victory or defeat, there is a peace that comes from God. He is our Banner.

We create banners for many earthly things; they hang or wave high, and they declare something with boldness. The Lord is our Banner. The Lord is our banner, that is not made of human hands. It is The Lord Himself, who is our Banner. We declare His love, strength, and control over us. He is the Banner over us.

The Lord was also the Israelites' Banner. In Exodus 13: 21 we read, "And the Lord went before them by day in a pillar of a cloud, to lead them the way; and by night in a pillar of fire, to give them light; to go by day and night:" He leads the way, when we are surrendered to His will. He goes before us, as The Lord our banner. Isaiah 52:12 says, "For you shall not go out with haste, nor go by flight; for the Lord will go before you, and the God of Israel will be your rear guard."

Just like with the Israelites, The Lord is always with us; He travels with us everywhere we go. He is a covering over us. He watches out for us, and keeps our paths straight, if we trust in Him. He leads the way in righteousness and Truth. Just like He led the Israelites with a cloud and fire, we have the Holy Spirit leading us.

The Lord is our Banner. The Lord leads us. He is our identifying marker. It is in The Lord, where all our faith, trust, and hope must lie. There is no other who is worthy, except our Lord and Savior, Jesus Christ. The Lord is our Banner.

~Love

Love is expressed, felt, and defined differently in the world than it is according to God's expression of love. To the world, "love" is more experiential, and at times, temporary. The word love is misused and abused in our everyday postmodern, humanist culture. We use the word very loosely, therefore our "love" is often canceled, or blotted out, based on feelings and circumstances. We tend to manipulate, overuse, and misunderstand the word love, and it loses its power and strength of conviction.

We declare our love for sushi, and ice cream. We say we love certain music, or genres of books. We love chocolate. We love the beach, and barbecues. We use the same word, love, when referring to our family members, or our spouse. We say we love God, as well as ice tea on a summer day. We have a plethora of words in our vocabulary to choose from. We must move away from the habit of declaring our love for just about anything.

Psychologists describe several different forms of love. Because of sin, natural affection and love have been tainted. The Greek word for brotherly love, is Phileo. Phileo love is based on similarities and platonic, non-familial relationships. The Greek word Eros, is given to express erotic or self-serving love. The Bible tells us that God is love, and true love comes from Him. He created man in His image, and therefore we all have the capacity to love appropriately. The Biblical, God ordained love, which is supernatural in nature, is Agape love.

As Christ followers, we must be mindful of our casual declaration of love. We must focus on the love of Christ, and not the kind of love propagated by the world. Through the power of the Holy Spirit working in and through us, we are able to offer the type of love that God has for us, and has put in the hearts of believers. This love of God is unconditional Agape love. This type of love is what God extends to us.

Authentic agape love is unconditional, selfless love, and it is graciously extended to all. According to God's will, we truly love with Agape love when we love without expectations, selfish motives, conditions, or limitations. It is perfectly demonstrated by Christ toward us. It is God's unconditional Agape love that caused Him to send Jesus to Earth to die as the payment for our sin. It is also demonstrated in His grace, mercy, and patience extended to us.

Love is not only an action, but also a choice. We show Agape love as a result of choosing it. God's love is perfect and pure, whereas, our expression of love is not perfect, but tarnished by our sin nature. Sin leaves a blemish on our ability to love. Hebrews 10:14 tells us, "For by one offering He has perfected forever those who are being sanctified." We are made righteous because of Christ. We are only able to love unconditionally, because of the Holy Spirit in us.

Our love for others is made new when we surrender our lives to Jesus Christ. We are capable of loving His way, because the love of Christ is in us. We are able to love unconditionally, because of Christ manifesting His Agape love through us. It is only because of Him that we are able to extend this love to others.

God's love is not an emotion or a feeling. Feelings and emotions are conditional, temporary, and are dependent upon our circumstances. Our emotions change. Our feelings cannot be trusted. Emotions and feelings are conscious mental reactions, based on our impression of circumstances. Biblical love is Agape love, which means it is unconditional. Biblical love is an action, driven by our obedience. Therefore, love is a choice. We choose through obedience to God, to love as He loves.

God is love. The Bible tells us in I John 4:8, "He that loveth not knoweth not God; for God is love." Additionally, I John 4:16 says, "**God is love**; and he that dwelleth in love dwelleth in God, and God in him." As born-again Christ followers, the Spirit of God dwells in our hearts. If the Holy Spirit dwells in us, so does His love.

Galatians 2:20 tells us, "I am crucified with Christ: nevertheless I live; yet not I, but Christ liveth in me: and the life which I now live in the flesh I live by the faith of the Son of God, who loved me, and gave himself for me." Knowing that Christ lives within us, we understand that Love lives within us. We understand what love actually is. We must pay attention, and not be drawn in by false, worldly representations of love.

Love is the person of God the Father, God the Son, and God the Holy Spirit. Romans 5:5 tells us, "And hope maketh not ashamed; because the love of God is shed abroad in our hearts by the Holy Ghost which is given unto us." As believers, God has placed love in our hearts. In John 14:20 Jesus says, "At that day ye shall know that I am in my Father, and ye in me, and I in you." I reiterate these truths, because they are essential for understanding what true love is, and knowing how to express authentic unconditional Christ like love.

The attributes of love are expressed in I Corinthians 13:4-8. It says, "Love suffers long *and* is kind; love does not envy; love does not parade itself, is not puffed up; does not behave rudely, does not seek its own, is not provoked, thinks no evil; does not rejoice in iniquity, but rejoices in the truth; bears all things, believes all things, hopes all things, endures all things. Love never fails (NKJV)." This is essentially the definition of Agape love found in God's Word.

Because God the Holy Spirit lives in us, and He is love; love is part of who we are, as Christ followers. It should be demonstrated in our lifestyle. We must choose to use, or activate this love that God has placed inside of us, His children. Otherwise, His love will lie dormant, compelling us to rely on the world's definition, our feelings, and our emotions, which are not trustworthy.

God is love. Love lives within us through the indwelling of His Holy Spirit. Be encouraged, and let Christ's love flow through you.

~Our Love For God

God, The Almighty One, is worthy of our love.

Sometimes we need to reflect on our relationship with God, and what it looks like to truly love Him. Specifically, we need to marvel at the reasons we love Him. Love is a choice, and it is demonstrative. How we express our love toward God is a direct response to how we understand, and experience the love God has for us. We must examine why we have chosen to love God. We must refrain from flippantly saying we love God, without any demonstration of that love.

When we think of the immeasurable love that God extends to us, it should cause us to reflect on the many reasons we love Him in return. In our earthly relationships, we often rehearse the reasons we love someone, especially if we are married. We often ponder what it was that made us fall in love, and what it is about that person that makes us continue loving them with the passage of time. From time to time, we all should take a moment to reminisce about what it is about our Lord and Savior, Jesus Christ, that makes us love Him.

We love Him because He has commanded it. In Exodus 20:3 God says, "Thou shalt have no other gods before me." In Mark 12:30 we read, "And thou shalt love the Lord thy God with all thy heart, and with all thy soul, and with all thy mind, and with all thy strength: this is the first commandment." God created us to love Him. Yes, God has commanded us to love Him, but we have to choose to do so.

We are told to love Him with everything within us; heart, soul, mind, and strength. This verse also can be referenced in Matthew 22:37-38 and Luke 10:27. God's first commandment is to love Him. Let us, in obedience, love God with our entire heart, which is our conscious as well as emotions. Let us, in obedience, love God with our soul which is our spirit, or inner man. Let's love Him with every breath that we take. Let us, in obedience, love God with our mind, which is our intellect. Let us, in obedience, love God with our strength, which is our power and ability.

We love Him because He first loved us, and we should find it impossible to resist the love God lavishes on us. I John 4:19 reads, "We love Him, because He first loved us." He loved us, even when we didn't acknowledge Him at all. Psalm 139:16 tells us, "Thine eyes did see my substance, yet being imperfect; and in thy book all my members were written, which in continuance were fashioned, when as yet there was none of them." When we come to realize that God knew us, and loved us before we took our first breaths, how could we do anything but love Him.

We love Him because He is faithful. Deuteronomy 7:9 tells us, "Know therefore that the Lord thy God, he is God, the faithful God, which keepeth covenant and mercy with them that love him and keep his commandments to a thousand generations." God, through the powerful working of His Holy Spirit, faithfully pursues our hearts, even when we continually resist. His eyes, His thoughts, and His love are faithfully upon us, even before we turn our affections toward Him. He is faithful.

We love Him because He draws us out of darkness, towards Himself. In Jeremiah 31: 3, he is speaking of Israel, but it applies to all generations, including us. "The Lord hath appeared of old unto me, saying, Yea, I have loved thee with an everlasting love: therefore, with lovingkindness have I drawn thee." We love Him for rescuing us from darkness. I Peter 2:9 says, "But ye are a chosen generation, a royal priesthood, a holy nation, a peculiar people; that ye should shew forth the praises of him who hath called you out of darkness into his marvelous light." God has called us to Himself, and we no longer are hidden in the darkness behind our sin and shame. God draws us to Himself.

We love Him because He gave His only son, Jesus, to die for our sins. Romans 5:8 says, "But God commendeth his love toward us, in that, while we were yet sinners, Christ died for us." We should consider the amazing sacrifice that God made for us. He did it out of His love for us. He sacrificed Jesus, so that we could be reconciled to Him. At the thought of this, our hearts should well up with gratitude and love. I John 4:10 tells us, "Herein is love, not that we loved God, but that he loved us, and sent his Son to be the propitiation for our sins." God's love is so great for us, that He used His very own son to bridge the gap between us.

Because of Jesus' blood shed on the cross, we can experience forgiveness, and be united in relationship with God. I John 1:9 says, "If we confess our sins, he is faithful and just to forgive us our sins, and to cleanse us from all unrighteousness." There is so much power behind the forgiveness that is granted to us by God. We love Him because He forgives us, and does not hold our sin over us. His forgiveness cleanses us, and affords us a fresh start. We love Him because He forgives us of our sins.

There are certain attributes of God's character that all believers love. There are things that we love about God, that are unique to our personal relationship with Him. Please examine your individual reasons for loving Him. We each have particular ways in which the Lord has touched our lives. We each have our own testimony of the goodness of God. We each have a personal connection with our Lord and Savior, Jesus Christ, that is exclusive to us.

One of the very many individual reasons I have for loving God, is the quickened response of the Holy Spirit that promoted instant change in me. Before I surrendered my life to The Lord in 1992, my biggest obstacle was my belief that I could not change, or be changed. I made numerous attempts to change my wretched behaviors, with zero success. In fact, some behaviors worsened with each trial.

When I accepted Jesus Christ as my Lord and Savior, God showed me His faithfulness, and instantly removed all of the behaviors that I was unsuccessful at changing on my own. I am not exaggerating when I say "all." I am not talking about dealing with consequences and shame, because that was more of a process. I am referring to all of my shameful behaviors that I identified with. They literally ceased to be part of my life. I never turned back.

Every desire to do any of the things that the former me did, disappeared. I believe in the power of God to change lives. Through the working of the Holy Spirit, and an authentically willing vessel, it can happen in an instant. I knew, and still know, that only God is able to change the "willing" heart of man. I love Him so much, beyond measure, for doing what I had no power to do. I will forever love, cherish, and stand in awe of my Heavenly Father.

God is worthy of our love, honor, and praise.

~El Roi: The God Who Sees

El Roi, the God who sees, is one of the many names of God. There is power and compassion in the name El Roi: The God who sees me. Our God sees you in and through every circumstance you face. He sees it all. Nothing goes undetected by God. In Genesis chapter 16, we meet Hagar. Abram and Sarai, (later named Abraham and Sarah), were advanced in age, and did not have any children. Sarai wanted a child, but she found it difficult to wait on the Lord.

Sarai had a handmaiden named Hagar, and she decided to use Hagar to fulfill this desire that had gone unmet. Sarai gave Hagar to Abram, so that through Hagar, she could have a child. Abram took Hagar as his wife, and she conceived. Hagar felt contempt toward Sarai, Abram's first wife, when she learned that she was with child. She resented Sarai. Sarai saw the disdain Hagar had for her, therefore, Sarai was harsh with Hagar. As a result, Hagar ran away.

The angel of the Lord appeared before Hagar, and told her to go back to Sarai and submit to her. The angel of the Lord told Hagar "go back," and deal with the issues. He told her that he would multiply her seed exceedingly. She was told she would have a son, and his name will be Ishmael, because the Lord heard her affliction. The Lord saw Hagar. He also sees you.

She was forewarned that her son would be trouble. After Hagar's encounter with the angel of the Lord, Hagar called the

Lord the God who sees me. El Roi means the God Who Sees Me. The only occurrence of God being called El Roi is found here in the sixteenth chapter of Genesis. You can be assured, that God sees you.

God saw Hagar when she was feeling dejected, hopeless, lonely, and used. He met her exactly where she was, and comforted her. God sees us exactly where we are, and offers us compassion, discipline, love, guidance, or whatever it is that He extends to us. God showed Hagar, as He shows us, that running from our problems offers us no resolution or restoration. God showed Hagar, just like He shows us, that He will be with us as we walk through and work through our pain and our triumphs. He sees us, and He comes along side of us. Every aspect of our lives matters to God.

God sees when we are traumatized. In Romans 12:19, He tells us, "Dearly beloved, avenge not yourselves, but rather give place unto wrath: for it is written, Vengeance is mine; I will repay, saith the Lord." God will deal with our oppressors whether through grace and mercy, or wrath. He will shoulder that burden for us. He loves us, and He sees us. He sees our affliction, and He heals us. He strengthens us.

Being named The God who Sees, El Roi, is fitting, and speaks to God's character. Hebrews 4:13 assures us, "Neither is there any creature that is not manifest in his sight: but all things are naked and opened unto the eyes of him with whom we have to do." God is omniscient; He knows everything. God is aware of everything: past, present, and future. Nothing escapes God's sight. He sees us. There is complete transparency with us when it comes to God. We have no other choice, but to be transparent. He is omnipresent. God is everywhere, and He sees all things.

Everything that has ever happened to us, is happening to us, and will happen to us, is seen by El Roi. Psalm 33:13 says,

"The Lord looketh from heaven; he beholdeth all the sons of men. From the place of his habitation he looketh upon all the inhabitants of the earth." He sees us. He knows all that we have endured, triumphed through, been successful at, and struggled through.

He was, and is, right there with us. Proverbs 15:3 tells us, "The eyes of the Lord are in every place, beholding the evil and the good." He sees us individually. His heart wells up with joy when He sees our victories, triumphs, and accomplishments. His heart breaks when He sees our disappointments, fears, trauma, and sorrow. He loves us. We are His beloved, and He sees us.

We can be comforted by the fact that our Loving God sees us. We can rejoice in knowing that He is with us every step of our journey. He cares for us deeply, and He is watching over us. El Roi never takes His gaze off of us.

God sees us.

~How God Sees Us

Let's think about how God sees us, and consider viewing ourselves through His eyes.

If we could only see ourselves as God sees us, it would not only transform our minds, but it would also be life altering. We have a tainted view of ourselves, because of the lies of the world, and the enemy of our souls, the devil. We attribute our negative views, and skewed perception of ourselves to our upbringing, past life circumstances, current life circumstances, and even words spoken over us. No one's opinion of us matters aside from God's.

We must accept, embrace, and believe the truth about how God sees us, once we surrender all of ourselves to Him. We must put our past behind us, and never look back. Focusing on the love and adoration that our Lord and Savior has for us, will help stifle the enemy's infiltration of our thoughts. Our lives would be enriched, and truly rewarding, if we would begin to see ourselves as our Lord and Savior, Jesus Christ, sees us. God desires that we see ourselves as He sees us.

God sees us as loved. God loves us. God loved us before we were even born. His love crosses all boundaries, and reaches to the greatest of sinners. He loves us so much, but our sin and unbelief separate us from God. The depth of His love is so intense, but He cannot lavish it upon us unless we repent and place our faith and trust in Christ. God draws us to Himself, but we must respond with a surrendered heart. He never stops loving, but those who reject Christ will spend eternity separated from the love of God. Those of us who love God in return will never be separated from His great love. God sees us as loved.

God sees us as righteous. When we place our faith and trust in Jesus Christ, we are instantly clothed in righteousness. We may not see ourselves as righteous, but He sees us that way. We may not always feel righteous, because of our sin; but if we know Him, He sees us as righteous, always. II Corinthians 5:21 says, "For he hath made him to be sin for us, who knew no sin; that we might be made the righteousness of God in him." God has imputed, or credited, righteousness to us, through the blood of Jesus Christ. It is a gift given, or placed on, repentant sinners. God no longer sees us as sinners, but as righteous. We, who place our faith in Him, are in right standing with our Lord and Savior, Jesus Christ. He sees us as righteous.

God sees us as His beloved children. Galatians 4: 6-7 tells us, "And because ye are sons, God hath sent forth the Spirit of his Son into your hearts, crying, Abba, Father. Wherefore thou art no more a servant, but a son; and if a son, then an heir of God through Christ." He has adopted us as sons and daughters the minute we surrender our lives to Him. We are the children of God.

He does not see who we use to be, because we died to our old selves so that Christ may live in and through us. I John 3:1 says, "Behold, what manner of love the Father hath bestowed upon us, that we should be called the sons of God: therefore, the world knoweth us not, because it knew him not." God loves us, we are His children, and we now can experience the adoration of the one and the only perfect Father. John 1:12

says, "But as many as received him, to them gave he power to become the sons of God, even to them that believe on his name:" We are God's children. God sees us as His children.

God sees us as sanctified. Hebrews 10:13 says, "For by one offering he hath perfected forever them that are sanctified" God sees us as set apart, for His good pleasure and for His glory. He calls us to a life of sanctification. We should live as consecrated for God's purposes and glory.

When we surrender our will for God's, He sees us as being sanctified daily. Sanctification is the process of becoming holy. This process will not end until we are in our heavenly bodies. I Corinthians 6:11 tells us, "And such were some of you: but ye are washed, but ye are sanctified, but ye are justified in the name of the Lord Jesus, and by the Spirit of our God." God sees us as being sanctified.

When we place our faith and trust in Jesus Christ, He no longer sees our sin. Colossians 2: 13-14 tells us, " And you, being dead in your sins and the uncircumcision of your flesh, hath he quickened together with him, having forgiven you all trespasses; Blotting out the handwriting of ordinances that was against us, which was contrary to us, and took it out of the way, nailing it to his cross;" He sees us as forgiven.

We are forgiven of all of our sins from the past, our present sins, and any sin that we may commit in the future. Psalm 32:1-2 says, "Blessed is he whose transgression is forgiven, whose sin is covered. Blessed is the man unto whom the LORD imputeth not iniquity, and in whose spirit there is no guile." The grace and mercy of God, covers our iniquities, and we are forgiven. God sees us as forgiven.

We can begin to truly see ourselves as God sees us, if we will believe Him. We must renounce the spirit of unbelief in our lives, and walk in His truth. Let's truly trust Him, and His Word concerning us. Once we dissolve the spirit of unbelief, and are overcome with a spirit of belief, we will be able to see ourselves as God sees us.

~Peace With God vs. The Peace Of God

There is a difference between being at peace with God, and having the peace of God.

Before we surrender our hearts and minds to Jesus, we are not at peace with God, nor do we have the peace of God within us. When we are not walking with the Lord; we are spiritually restless. Although we may claim to be at peace, we actually have no real idea what that means until we surrender our all to Our Lord and Savior, Jesus Christ. It is then that we begin to experience authentic peace that only God can provide.

Before we accept Jesus as our personal Savior, we are not at peace with God. If the manner in which we live our lives aligns with the world's expectations, standards, and values, we are in direct opposition to God's Word, and God's will. James 4:4 says, "know ye not that the friendship of the world is enmity with God? whosoever therefore will be a friend of the world is the enemy of God." Enmity with God means in opposition to His ways.

There are a few things that must take place within our hearts and minds before we experience peace with God. First, we must recognize, and admit that we are sinners. Secondly, we must believe that Jesus died, was buried, and rose again for our sins. Next, we must ask Jesus to forgive us for sinning against Him. Lastly, we must accept His free gift of salvation.

When we have done these things, we immediately have peace with God.

Romans 5:1-2 tells us, "Therefore, since we have been justified through faith, we have peace with God through our LORD Jesus Christ, through whom we have gained access by faith into this grace in which we now stand. And we boast in the hope of the glory of God." We are justified. We are reconciled with Christ; His Holy Spirit is in us, and we have peace with God when we place our faith and trust in Him. Our status will never change, because our salvation is secure, and so is the peace we now have with God.

When we have the peace of God, Philippians 4:6-7 says, "Be careful for nothing; but in everything by prayer and supplication with thanksgiving let your requests be made known unto God. And the peace of God, which passeth all understanding, shall keep your hearts and minds through Christ Jesus."

The peace of God is a calm and assurance that we have when we are fully trusting the Lord in all things. When we doubt, our peace of God is not there. When we are giving everything to the Lord in prayer, believing that He is in control, and truly resting in His promises, we experience the peace of God in our hearts and minds. Experiencing the peace Of God is definitely contingent on our heart's posture toward the Lord.

We are human, and there are times when being human gets the best of us. We worry, get anxious, try to handle things on our own. We forget that God is sovereign. It is when we do these things that the peace of God retreats. The peace of God that rests in our hearts and minds is dependent on our obedience. On the other hand, peace with God never changes. If we have placed our faith and hope in the blood of Jesus, we have permanent, and unshakable peace with God.

~Tear Down The High Places

If we desire to honor God in all we do, we must tear down the high places. It is critical that we dismantle the throne of our hearts, and put God back in His rightful place.

In Biblical times, rebellion often presented itself through the worshipping of idols. Many people of that time were polytheistic, and worshiped many false gods. They would worship things created by human hands. Carved images were supposed to represent gods, as were golden statues.

Exodus 20:3-5 says, "Thou shalt have no other gods before me. Thou shalt not make unto thee any graven image, or any likeness of anything that is in heaven above, or that is in the earth beneath, or that is in the water under the earth. Thou shalt not bow down thyself to them, nor serve them: for I the Lord thy God am a jealous God, visiting the iniquity of the fathers upon the children unto the third and fourth generation of them that hate me;" There is one God: always has been, and always will be.

God has always despised idol worship of any kind. He mentions the tearing down of the high places where idol worship took place over one hundred times in the Bible. We are to worship Almighty God, only. Leviticus 26:30 says, "And I will destroy your high places, and cut down your images, and cast your carcases upon the carcases of your idols, and my soul shall abhor you."

He demanded the destruction of idols, and high places all throughout the Old testament. Numbers 33:52 says, "Then ye shall drive out all the inhabitants of the land from before you, and destroy all their pictures, and destroy all their molten images, and quite pluck down all their high places." These high places were where they burned incense, sacrificed, and worshipped foreign gods. The worship of Canaanite gods and idols took place because people wanted to "see" what they worshipped. They were drawn into idol worship, and it continued to further separate man from God. They had trouble placing their faith and trust in Almighty God, who is unseen.

Although our idol worship looks differently today, we still, as believers, tend to place other things where God's place should be in our hearts, minds, and lives. We must destroy the "high places" in our lives, which is any and all things that we tend to prioritize above our relationship with our Lord and Savior, Jesus Christ. This includes work, church, entertainment, relationships, our children, our spouses, material possessions, hobbies, or anything else that has taken God's rightful position in our lives.

These are idols that we have in today's self-centered culture. They may not be physical statues, or other "gods," but they are certainly idols, nonetheless. Colossians 3:2 says, "Set your affection on things above, not on things on the earth." It is important that we identify these idols that we have, in order to be in right relationship with our Lord and Savior, Jesus Christ.

When we think of idols, we may only imagine some type of statue or inanimate object. That is certainly how an idol can be presented, but think of things created by God that can become idols for believers. Remember, idols are things, people, activities, or anything that we put in God's place.

Romans 1:25 says, "Who changed the truth of God into a lie, and worshipped and served the creature more than the Creator, who is blessed forever. Amen." If there is anything in our lives that take the position that God should have in our lives, it is an idol for us. We must examine our hearts, and make certain that nothing is taking God's place on the throne of our hearts and lives.

Some things that have become idols for us may need to be eliminated from our lives. Other things that definitely must remain (like family, spouse, children, job, and so on), need to be reprioritized. Mark 12:30 tells us, "And thou shalt love the Lord thy God with all thy heart, and with all thy soul, and with all thy mind, and with all thy strength: this is the first commandment."

If we truly love God with our whole heart, and are fully immersed in our relationship with Him, we will recognize if anyone or anything is beginning to take more of our heart than God. There is nothing that we should love more than Him. God must remain on the throne of our hearts and our lives. Blessing will come, when we faithfully obey, and keep God first.

We must identify what, if anything, we are pouring more of ourselves into, than God. We must search our hearts and determine if there is anything that we desire more than our Lord and Savior, Jesus Christ. In Matthew 22:37 it says, "Jesus said unto him, Thou shalt love the Lord thy God with all thy heart, and with all thy soul, and with all thy mind." If there is anything at all that we can identify that we have put in God's place, it must abdicate the throne of our hearts. In order to live our lives in alignment with the will of God, we must place God back on the throne. He will not share the throne with another thing, person, or idea. Go ahead, tear down the high places.

~Sanctification

When we ask Jesus to be Lord of our lives, we are instantly made right with God, seen as righteous in His eyes, and have peace with Him. I John 1:9 assures us, "If we confess our sins, he is faithful and just to forgive us *our* sins, and to cleanse us from all unrighteousness."

Our identity is now in Christ. Colossians 3:3 says, "**For ye are dead, and your life is hid with Christ in God.**" This is salvation, that Christ died to pay our sin debt, and we must believe upon His name. As a result of our belief, we are saved from the penalty of sin, which is eternal separation from God. Although, our sins are instantly forgiven, and we are adopted into the Kingdom of God, we are far from perfect. We are not perfect, but we are perfectly justified.

Because we place our faith and trust in Jesus, we are instantly justified, or deemed righteous, by God. A result of God declaring us justified, or righteous, is that we are now absolved for our sin. We are free from guilt and blame. Acts 3:19 says, "Repent ye therefore, and be converted, that your sins may be blotted out, when the times of refreshing shall come from the presence of the Lord." We don't want to stop here. We want to experience growth in our relationship with Christ. We are now set apart, ready to develop our relationship, and accomplish God's will for our lives.

It is imperative that we actively get to know our Lord and Savior, Jesus Christ. To know Him, is to love him. To love Him, is to desire to please Him. To be set apart, and to grow in our faith, we must be active in our relationship with the Lord. We must study the Word of God, pray, and be clothed in Christ. In order to know and understand the ways of the Lord, we have to spend time with Him. John 17:17 says, "Sanctify them through thy truth: thy word is truth."

As we grow in our relationship with the Lord, we should become more and more like Christ. This continuing process of becoming holy, is called sanctification. Sanctification is referring to the spiritual growth that takes place through the working of the Holy Spirit of God in the lives of Christians. It is what is happening as we continually abandon, die to, and forsake, our flesh. II Corinthians 5:17 tells us, "Therefore if any man be in Christ, he is a new creature: old things are passed away; behold, all things are become new." Sanctification begins at salvation, and ends when we see Him face to face.

How the process of sanctification works:

The Holy Spirit indwells us when we surrender our hearts and minds to Christ. The Holy Spirit of God begins an ongoing, transformative work in our lives. The process of sanctification is the lifelong process of the Holy Spirit's presence in our lives: shaping our character, transforming our minds, healing our hearts, restructuring our priorities, restoring the damage caused by sin, and realigning our lives with God's plan and purpose for us.

When we surrender our lives to the Lord, we are not alone. We are unable to glorify God on our own. The Holy Spirit of God indwells all believers. Romans 8:11 tells us, "But if the Spirit of him that raised up Jesus from the dead dwell in you, he that raised up Christ from the dead shall also quicken your mortal bodies by his Spirit that dwelleth in you." It is the Holy Spirit that sanctifies us.

The Holy Spirit is the catalyst for our sanctification. Therefore, we must actively participate in the process, and not resist what the Holy Spirit is doing and producing in us. Through this process of sanctification, we will experience ongoing spiritual growth, renewal of our minds, and our lives will maintain alignment with God's will. This requires us to be willing. We must surrender our will, for God's. When we do, The Holy Spirit is free to transform our lives.

We are no longer conformed to the world; our minds are renewed. We are being transformed from the inside out, and we are now able to prove what is that good, and acceptable, and perfect will of God. Our desires become God's desires. We desire His will to be done in our lives. This is all the result of Christ saving us, redeeming us, and giving us new life in Christ. I Peter 2:9 tells us that He has called us, or rescued us from the darkness of the world, and has brought us into His marvelous light. Let the process of sanctification continually draw you closer to our Lord and Savior, Jesus Christ.

God is patient, yet persistent, through the process, and we must be as well.

~Part 2

Part two is comprised of writings designed to give us a better understanding of our responsibilities as ambassadors for Jesus, here on earth. These writings are intended to demonstrate how the Holy Spirit of God relentlessly pursues us, and transforms us.

Part two also serves as a guide to living consecrated lives that are set apart to honor and glorify our Heavenly Father. Part two will serve to remind us of the love God has for us, and how we ought to respond to His love. To know Him, is to love Him. To love Him, is to bring glory and honor to Him.

Be encouraged, we are not on this journey alone.

~Newness In Christ

The very moment we surrender our lives to Jesus, our old self dies, and we are made spiritually new in Christ. What takes place the moment we ask Jesus to be Lord of our lives is a supernatural miracle. This moment marks the beginning of our lifelong sanctification process, or the process of becoming more like Jesus. We must continually die to our flesh, and allow Christ to manifest Himself in and through our lives.

Whether we live our lives in the fullness of all that we now possess, and allow the Holy Spirit to manifest Himself through us, is completely up to us. We still have free will, and must forsake our will, for the will of God in our lives. In order to walk fully adorned in our new identity in Christ, we must be active participants in the plan and purpose that the Lord sets before us.

God will do a complete overhaul of our lives by thoroughly and consistently renewing us for his glory. II Corinthians 5:17 says, "Therefore if any man be in Christ, he is a new creature: old things are passed away; behold, all things are become new." Let's study the components of II Corinthians 5:17, to better understand the life changing significance of our salvation.

"Therefore, if any man be in Christ:"

The word therefore, means as a result of something. "If" is a conditional word; so this first part of the verse, "If any man be in Christ," must be met in order for the rest of the verse to be true. The positioning words "in Christ," indicate that our relationship with God has been restored through the shed blood of Jesus Christ, and we are reunited with Him.

We have a new position in life, and a new purpose. Prior to this, sin had separated us from God. We are now grafted "in," and we are intimately connected to Christ the moment we accept Jesus Christ as our personal Savior. John 15:5 says, "I am the vine, ye are the branches: He that abideth in me, and I in him, the same bringeth forth much fruit: for without me ye can do nothing."

If we are "in Christ," we are no longer separated from Him. We are in relationship with Him. He becomes our lifeline, so to speak. The Holy Spirit of God comes to dwell in us. Romans 8:11 says, "But if the Spirit of him that raised up Jesus from the dead dwell in you, he that raised up Christ from the dead shall also quicken your mortal bodies by his Spirit that dwelleth in you." We are in the family of Christ. Romans 12:5 tells us, "So we, being many, are one body in Christ, and every one members one of another."

"He is a new creature:"

When we surrender our lives to the Lordship of Jesus Christ, accepting His payment for our sins, and leaving our past behind, we are a new creature. Our former self dies, and we become new spiritually. We are no longer who we used to be. Romans 6:4 tells us, "Therefore we are buried with him by baptism into death: that like as Christ was raised up from the dead by the glory of the Father, even so we also should walk in newness of life." We put away our old self, and put on Christ.

We are made new because Christ now dwells in us. Galatians 3:27 says, "For as many of you as have been baptized into Christ have put on Christ." Now that we are "in Christ," we have done away with our old sinful self. We are a new creature, because of our acceptance of Christ's redemptive work on the cross. As new creatures in Christ, we still have a sinful nature, but we are no longer controlled by our flesh. We no longer obey our flesh, and when we fail, there is grace and mercy, and Christ has already forgiven us.

"old things are passed away:"

As new creatures, sin no longer is our master, and we must no longer identify with the things of the past. This is not a suggestion, but necessary. If we cling to our past, we are unable to fully live in the freedom of our new life in Christ. Romans 6:6 says, "Knowing this, that our old man is crucified with him, that the body of sin might be destroyed, that henceforth we should not serve sin."

When we surrender our lives to Christ, we die to our old self. We put our old self to death, so that Christ may live in and through us. Galatians 5:24 tells us, "And they that are Christ's have crucified the flesh with the affections and lusts."

You are "in Christ." You are a new creature. In order to experience this newness of life, old things must pass away. We can no longer identify with our former selves. Who we used to be, is dead. It is critical that we refrain from resurrecting the former self, who has died. We must stop looking back, and look forward to our new life which is hidden in Christ Jesus. Our old selves are no longer welcome, and we must deny any attempts of our flesh, or the enemy of our souls, to resurrect our old self. We have power, through the Holy Spirit of God, to keep the dead man dead.

"behold, all things are become new:"

The word "become," indicates that our newness in Christ is also a process. We continually die to self, as all things become new. As we grow in our walk with the Lord, some aspects of our new life gradually change as we mature. Some changes are instantaneous, such as our identity, but other areas change as God prunes and shapes us into His likeness. Philippians 1:6 says, "Being confident of this very thing, that he which hath begun a good work in you will perform it until the day of Jesus Christ:" As we yearn after the things of God, and God reveals truth to us, we become more like Him.

Christ lives in us, and our old self is no longer welcome. Galatians 2:20 says, "I am crucified with Christ: nevertheless, I live; yet not I, but Christ liveth in me: and the life which I now live in the flesh I live by the faith of the Son of God, who loved me, and gave himself for me." We are regenerated, or born again in the spirit.

We died to our old selves, and we are regenerated, and made alive in Christ. Titus 3:5 says, "Not by works of righteousness which we have done, but according to his mercy he saved us, by the washing of regeneration, and renewing of the Holy Ghost." When all things become new, we forsake the old. We no longer walk in darkness, because we have been rescued, set free, and now walk in the light of the Lord.

It is a miraculous transformation that takes place when we accept what Christ did on the cross to redeem us. God is good, and those of us who are born again, can testify of our transformed lives. No one but Almighty God is capable of such things. Romans 6:3-4 says, "Know ye not, that so many of us as were baptized into Jesus Christ were baptized into his death? Therefore, we are buried with him by baptism into death: that like as Christ was raised up from the dead by the glory of the Father, even so we also should walk in newness of life." If your identity is in Christ, you are a new creature; the old has passed away, and thank Jesus, that all things are become new.

~Set Apart For God's Glory

We were created by God, for God. We are meant to be consecrated, or set apart for God's honor and glory.

When we meditate on what it means to be set apart, we must immediately think of Jesus. We must consider what His desire is for us, and what it looks like to bring glory and honor to Him. To be set apart doesn't necessarily mean that our goal is to physically look, or appear to look, strikingly different than our worldly counterparts. Outward appearances can be deceptive; it is our heart's posture toward our Heavenly Father that generates authentic, God- honoring change.

The Word of God is clear when it says that we are not to conform to the world. The Word of God is also clear when it tells us that our purpose is to do the will of God, and bring glory to Him. This is not optional for those who have placed their faith and trust in Almighty God. When we surrender our hearts and minds to Jesus, we are consecrated, or set apart. It is now up to us, how we represent the Lord.

We are not to conform to the world. John tells us what the "world" is, in I John. I John 2:16 says, "For all that is in the world, the lust of the flesh, and the lust of the eyes, and the pride of life, is not of the Father, but is of the world." We are new creations in Christ; therefore, we are not to live our lives, or think, according to the standards of our culture, or of the world. We should not want to, if we are clothed in Christ. Romans 13:14 says, "But put ye on the Lord Jesus Christ, and make not provision for the flesh, to fulfil the lusts thereof."

We must not come into agreement with what the world has determined is right and acceptable. We are no longer in covenant with the world. We dissolved our covenant with our flesh, the devil, and this world. James 4:4 says, "Ye adulterers and adulteresses, know ye not that the friendship of the world is enmity with God? Whosoever therefore will be a friend of the world is the enemy of God." We are now in an eternal covenant with our Lord and Savior, Jesus Christ. We must be set apart.

We are now in covenant, or agreement, with our Lord and Savior, Jesus Christ. We will no longer uphold the expectations of this world for living, thinking, and behaving. I John 2:15 tells us plainly, "Love not the world, neither the things that are in the world. If any man love the world, the love of the Father is not in him."

We must forsake the ways of the world, and allow Christ's love to manifest through us. We can forsake the ways of the world without arrogance, pride, or disdain toward those who are plagued by the spirit of unbelief. Remember, we are set apart, and God may choose to use us to usher someone from the stronghold of unbelief, into the freedom found in faith and belief in Jesus.

We have the power of the Holy Spirit within us, to guide our thoughts, words, and actions. Galatians 2:20 says, "I am crucified with Christ: nevertheless I live; yet not I, but Christ liveth in me: and the life which I now live in the flesh I live by the faith of the Son of God, who loved me, and gave himself for me." The way we live our lives should no longer fall into alignment with the pattern of the world. We have a new mind in Christ. We are consecrated, set apart, for the Lord's purpose and plan. Consecration happens the moment we surrender our lives to Christ. We are set apart.

When non-believers see us, spend time with us, or watch us, they should see Jesus. When we are set apart, we no longer blend in with the world. Never forget our purpose, which is to bring glory to God. Jesus must be seen in us, to authentically share the Gospel message with others. Jesus must be evident in all we say and do. We are in the world as Christ's voice, hands, and feet.

Christ wants us to love Him and His Word. The world should no longer have any enticing power over us. We must let our light shine before men, and influence the world for Jesus. Matthew 5:14-16 tells us, "Ye are the light of the world. A city that is set on a hill cannot be hid. Neither do men light a candle, and put it under a bushel, but on a candlestick; and it giveth light unto all that are in the house. Let your light so shine before men, that they may see your good works, and glorify your Father which is in heaven."

We must be the influencers, and not be influenced by the world. I Peter 2:9 tells us that He has called us, or rescued us from the darkness of the world, and has brought us into His marvelous light. If we are set apart, our lives will point others to Jesus, the Way Maker, Miracle Worker, and Life Changer.

We have everything we require through the power of the Holy Spirit living in us, to be set apart. The devil has lied to us, stolen from us, and destroyed enough. We have been rescued from his dominion. We have been rescued from the grip of sin and death. We must not go back and indulge in any way in the darkness of the world, but we must let Jesus shine into the darkness, through us. Let go of the world, and truly be consecrated; be set apart. Let Jesus be seen in you.

~Durable Faith

Who we are in Christ, is a result of our faith. As Christians, our lives are lived by faith in our Lord and Savior, Jesus Christ, and what He did for us on the cross at Calvary. Our faith changed us from unrighteous to righteous in the eyes of the Lord. Romans 1:17 says, "For therein is the righteousness of God revealed from faith to faith: as it is written, the just shall live by faith." We are made righteous in God's eyes, because of our faith.

We are justified, or made righteous, because of our faith in Christ. Philippians 3:9 tells us further, "And be found in him, not having mine own righteousness, which is of the law, but that which is through the faith of Christ, the righteousness which is of God by faith." It is because of our faith, that we are made right with God. Hebrews 12:2 tells us, "Looking unto Jesus the author and finisher of our faith; who for the joy that was set before him endured the cross, despising the shame, and is set down at the right hand of the throne of God." Our faith, because of Christ's finished work on the cross, must be durable.

It is critical for us to possess faith that is immovable, and rock solid. Our faith in our Lord and Savior, Jesus Christ, must be able to withstand any circumstances that come our way. Our faith, should be firmly rooted in truth, and the fact that God's promises are reliable. Hebrews 11:1 tells us what faith is, when it says, "Now faith is the substance of things hoped for, the evidence of things not seen." We must be grounded, and secure in our faith.

There are many things that we may not be able to see, touch, or even fully understand about God; but through faith, we believe and we will not be moved. II Corinthians 5:7 says, "For we walk by faith, not by sight." We must maintain that circumstances are temporary, but our faith is everlasting. Durable faith is present, through all of the circumstances of life.

Life comes at us fast. There are many unpredictable circumstances that we will face, and we must be ready to meet them with unwavering faith in Jesus Christ. James 1:6 says, "But let him ask in faith, nothing wavering. For he that wavereth is like a wave of the sea driven with the wind and tossed." If we have durable faith, we will come before the Lord, and ask anything according to His will, and have faith that His answer will be in our best interest.

Regardless of how things appear, we must resolve that God is in control, and our faith in Him will remain firm. Hebrews 11:6 tells us, "But without faith it is impossible to please him: for he that cometh to God must believe that he is, and that he is a rewarder of them that diligently seek him." Durable faith comes from unshakable belief that Our Lord and Savior, Jesus Christ, is exactly who He says He is. Durable faith is imperative for believers.

Our faith in God, must be able to stand up against the ungodliness of the world and the godless views that bombard us. What the world propagates should not alter our faith. Ungodliness and ever-changing standards of this world are temporary, but our faith must be able to withstand through it all. I John 1:4 tells us, "For whatsoever is born of God overcometh the world: and this is the victory that overcometh the world, even our faith." Our faith must be impenetrable. Nothing that takes place in this world, or the standards set by the world, should be capable of shaking our faith in Almighty God. This is durable faith.

Durable faith comes from knowing God, and being known by Him. Our faith will only be durable if we are walking closely with the Lord, and studying His Word. Romans 10:17 says, "So then faith cometh by hearing, and hearing by the word of God." Keep God's Word in your heart, and walk by faith. May your faith be durable.

~The Proverbs 31 Woman

You may be surprised that you are well on your way to modeling the characteristics of the Proverbs 31 woman. This is not just for women, because men can learn volumes as well.

When we read Proverbs 31:10-31, most women are overcome with feelings of inadequacy. We look at the wording, and think that these verses no longer apply to us. Every word of the Bible applies to us. Some so-called independent women may even scoff at the entire passage.

I will admit that in the past, I have viewed these verses as unattainable. I wasn't allowing the Holy Spirit to show me that every woman, regardless of the era they live in, can be this woman of virtue, honor, strength, and integrity. I formerly thought that I could never reach the level of virtue, as the woman described in these verses. This is a lie, and we will dismantle this lie from the author of lies, the devil. All women are capable of being a Proverbs 31 woman of God.

She is the picture of the ideal wife. She is described as an "excellent," or "virtuous" wife, mother, and woman of God. Keep in mind, that she is not "perfect," but she is "excellent," and "virtuous." Who could ever reach this level of spiritual greatness? We know that there is no one on this earth who is perfect, because Jesus Christ is the only one who is perfect.

We do not evolve; God created us in His image, and we have always been women. Our desires, longings, the way we love, our thoughts, our tendencies, our sinful nature, and everything else that makes us women, has never changed. What we face in humanity, is nothing new. Ecclesiastes 1: 9 says, "The thing that hath been, it is that which shall be; and that which is done is that which shall be done: and there is no new thing under the sun." Let's not shy away from learning from Proverbs 31, but instead, let's examine how we can apply the principles and practices of this woman of utmost virtue, to our own lives.

Carefully read through the following verses.

Proverbs 31: 10-31 reads, "Who can find a virtuous woman? for her price is far above rubies. The heart of her husband doth safely trust in her, so that he shall have no need of spoil. She will do him good and not evil all the days of her life. She seeketh wool, and flax, and worketh willingly with her hands. She is like the merchants' ships; she bringeth her food from afar. She riseth also while it is yet night, and giveth meat to her household, and a portion to her maidens. She considereth a field, and buyeth it: with the fruit of her hands she planteth a vineyard. She girdeth her loins with strength, and strengtheneth her arms. She perceiveth that her merchandise is good: her candle goeth not out by night. She layeth her hands to the spindle, and her hands hold the distaff. She stretcheth out her hand to the poor; yea, she reacheth forth her hands to the needy. She is not afraid of the snow for her household: for all her household are clothed with scarlet. She maketh herself coverings of tapestry; her clothing is silk and purple. Her husband is known in the gates, when he sitteth among the elders of the land. She maketh fine linen, and selleth it; and delivereth girdles unto the merchant. Strength and honour are her clothing; and she shall rejoice in time to come. She openeth her mouth with wisdom; and in her tongue is the law of kindness. She looketh well to the ways of her household, and eateth not the bread of idleness. Her children arise up, and call her blessed; her husband also, and he praiseth her. Many daughters have done virtuously, but thou excellest them all. Favour is deceitful, and beauty is vain: but a woman that feareth the LORD, she shall be praised. Give her of the fruit of her hands; and let her own works praise her in the gates."

As we read through these verses, we must be careful not to take on a prideful attitude. We must not allow the devil to deceive us into believing that these characteristics don't apply to women today. They certainly do. The world does not ascribe to Godly standards, God ordained gender roles, or guidelines for righteousness.

God has never changed His expectations for His children. He does not change with the changing times, and cultural expectations. Hebrews 13:8 tells us, "Jesus Christ the same yesterday, and today, and forever." These verses are priceless, and apply to every aspect of our lives today.

As we grow in God's grace and mercy, God transforms us. I Corinthians 15:10 says, "But by the grace of God I am what I am: and his grace which was bestowed upon me was not in vain; but I labored more abundantly than they all: yet not I, but the grace of God which was with me." Through obedience, we allow the Holy Spirit of God to align our hearts and our minds to the call He has placed on us.

As our heart's posture is increasingly stayed on Christ, we are being molded into the women of God, that He desires us to be. Becoming a Proverbs 31 woman is less about what we do, and more about who we are in Christ. It is more about our humility and our willingness to submit to our Lord and Savior, Jesus Christ.

Titus 2:4-5 tells us, "That they may teach the young women to be sober, to love their husbands, to love their children, to be discreet, chaste, keepers at home, good, obedient to their own husbands, that the word of God be not blasphemed."

When we, as women, fully surrender our will, for God's, we will become His version of the Proverbs 31 woman, that He desires us to be. Psalm 143:10 says, "Teach me to do Your will, For You are my God; Let Your good Spirit lead me on level ground." Every attribute of the Proverbs 31 woman may not directly apply to all women. For instance, if you are not married, these attributes can manifest themselves in other close relationships. Let's take a look at the characteristics of the Proverbs 31 woman.

A virtuous woman, will have the trust of her husband. He will safely, and easily give her his all, because she is a woman who loves the Lord. He is secure in their relationship, because he knows she walks closely with Jesus. She places God in His rightful place, which is first in her life. In Matthew 22:37 Jesus says, "Jesus said unto him, Thou shalt love the Lord thy God with all thy heart, and with all thy soul, and with all thy mind." Because of this, her husband's heart is overwhelmed with love, honor, and respect for her.

She only wants what is best for her husband, and seeks to do well by him, her entire life. The circumstances of life, will not change this for her. She builds her husband up, and supports his walk with the Lord. She encourages him, and loves him through the hills and valleys of their life together. Although no relationship is perfect, she is by his side through it all. She is wholly committed to God, and to her husband.

The virtuous woman of God is not deterred by the idea of hard work. She works diligently to provide for her family. She is not lazy. She is resourceful, and helps her husband with the running of the household. She is mindful and thoughtfully keeps their home in order. She is not resistant to putting the needs of her family before her own needs. She is selfless, and her life exhibits authentic joy in keeping her home in order. Whether she is a stay at home mom, self-employed, a business owner, a blue-collar worker, a career woman, etc., she has a clear perspective.

She gives her all to benefit her family. Our heavenly Father is her boss, not an earthly employer, or business. Colossians 3:23-24 says, "And whatsoever ye do, do it heartily, as to the LORD, and not unto men; Knowing that of the LORD ye shall receive the reward of the inheritance: for ye serve the LORD Christ." If her work is outside of the home, she does not allow her work to come before her family. She does not neglect her husband or her family. At the same time, she is innovative, and creatively makes a way to be helpful. Her heart is focused on Christ, her husband, her family. She keeps her priorities in alignment with the Lord's priorities.

The virtuous woman is mindful of the needs of others. In John 13:35 Jesus says, "By this shall all men know that ye are my disciples, if ye have love one to another." She has the heart and mind of Christ. She is sensitive to the those that she comes in contact with. She is generous, and kind. She is willing to help others who are less fortunate, without being judgmental. Her purpose is to show the love of Christ, and to be a living testimony of His grace and mercy.

The virtuous woman is blessed with Godly wisdom and discernment. James 1:5 says, "If any of you lack wisdom, let him ask of God, that giveth to all men liberally, and upbraideth not; and it shall be given him." She has Christ at the center of her life, and she allows Him to fill her with wisdom. She is not interested in what the world has to offer her, but only what the Lord has for her. Her heart's posture is forever before God. She pauses before she speaks, prays before she proceeds, and seeks counsel from the Lord always.

The virtuous woman is intentional, and is motivated by purpose. All that she does, all that she lives for, all that pushes her forward, is faithful obedience to Christ. She is not a busy body, aimlessly trying to figure things out as she goes. She is connected to Christ, and the heart and mind of Jesus is woven into the fabric of her being. She is led by the Holy Spirit of God; in all she is and in all she does. There is no compromising her walk with the Lord. She allows the Holy Spirit of God, to manifest Himself through her. She is not resistant to His presence in her life, and it is evident in the life that she leads.

Let us resist striving for perfection, because it is unattainable. Instead, allow God, through the power of His Holy Spirit, to work His perfect will in and through us.

~ Your Treasure Will Reveal Your Heart

Sometimes, we do not recognize when our priorities are out of alignment with the will of God. It is good practice to examine where our treasure is stored, and the spiritual impact it has on our lives from time to time.

Everyone is familiar with the cliché: "You can't take it with you." As overused as it is, it is a Biblical principle that is too often overlooked in practice. As believers, we are not called to store up treasures on this earth. What did Jesus mean when He said this? He is not saying that having a good job, earning a great salary, owning a house, and having a 401k, etc., are bad. No, He is warning that if our focus is on these things, our focus is no longer on Him.

Matthew 6:21 says, "For where your treasure is, there will your heart be also." This is a powerful verse, that calls for an examination of the heart. Our heart is a snapshot of what our desires and longings are, what our focus is, what we are committed to, and where we place our devotion.

Your heart will be where your treasure is. When God surveys our hearts, this is what He will find. There is no way around it, so let's not believe the lie of the enemy that says we can have our heart in two places. Jeremiah 17:10 says, "I the Lord search the heart, I try the reins, even to give every man according to his ways, and according to the fruit of his doings." Let us cling to and value what is eternal and precious to the Lord, and give worldly possessions and wealth their proper place.

Our Heavenly Father wants good things for His children. He provides every good thing. James 1:17 tells us," Every good gift and every perfect gift is from above, and cometh down from the Father of lights, with whom is no variableness, neither shadow of turning." If we allow Jesus to manage our earthly estate, as well as our Kingdom of God estate, it will all look like Kingdom treasure.

The Lord does not want earthly treasures to become our god. Matthew 6:19 says, "Lay not up for yourselves treasures upon earth, where moth and rust doth corrupt, and where thieves break through and steal:" Keeping our priorities properly ordered is a struggle that requires Jesus being on the throne of our lives, and a Godly mindset, to overcome.

Tangible possessions and monetary wealth can become obsessions and idols. Our hearts must be in constant pursuit of God, and we must keep a Godly perspective in all things. We must understand that earthly possessions and wealth do not last. Possessions break, wear out, get old, and can be stolen. Money can be lost or stolen. There is no permanent value or hope in either. This is why our earthly treasures must be treated as God's. After all, it all belongs to Him.

Peace will not be our portion if we are simultaneously pursuing worldly gain, and Jesus. It does not work. Matthew 6:24 tells us, "No man can serve two masters: for either he will hate the one, and love the other; or else he will hold to the one, and despise the other. Ye cannot serve God and mammon." If we maintain a Kingdom perspective, and remember from whom we are gifted all things, earthly things will not become our focus.

Our world places great esteem and honor upon the shoulders of those who have an abundance of wealth and material possessions. God, on the other hand, is not a respecter of persons. Acts 10: 34-35 says, "Then Peter opened his mouth, and said, of a truth I perceive that God is no respecter of persons: But in every nation he that feareth him, and worketh righteousness, is accepted with him."

He places value on our heart's posture toward Him. What matters to The Lord is a heart and mind stayed on, and surrendered to Him. What our treasure is will be reflected in what we are most devoted to. Colossians 3:2 tells us, "Set your affection on things above, not on things on the earth."

Now, as for treasures in heaven, there is nothing else that will receive any eternal value. When we sow into the Kingdom of God, and commit our lives to glorifying God, this is how we lay up treasures in heaven. Nothing can destroy, steal, or corrupt these treasures. Matthew 6:20 says, "But lay up for yourselves treasures in heaven, where neither moth nor rust doth corrupt, and where thieves do not break through nor steal:"

When our life ambition is to serve God, these eternal treasures in heaven will be a natural result. It is only If we have placed our faith and trust in Jesus, that we are able to store up our treasure in heaven.

We store up heavenly treasure through loving Jesus, sharing the Gospel, helping others, loving people, giving, forgiving, etc. If our treasures are in heaven, the monetary and tangible blessings can take their proper place. We must treat these as secondary blessings, which come from our Lord and Savior, Jesus Christ.

What kind of treasures are you storing: heavenly, or earthly?

Goal: Treasures in heaven.

~Submission

When we come to the realization that God is all powerful, all knowing, and almighty, we want to yield to His authority. Submission to the Lord God Almighty is critical in the life of someone who has placed their faith and trust in Jesus. Pride gets in the way of walking closely with God in total obedience and submission.

We think of someone having physical, psychological, and emotional control over another person when we hear the word submission. We are concerned that we will lose our voice if we are called to submit. We are concerned that we will no longer have input if we submit. In all actuality, submission to God is just another way of saying that we have surrendered to God. God calls us into submission to His will and His ways when we give our lives to Him.

Submission is defined in Oxford's dictionary as the action of accepting or yielding to a superior force or to the will or authority of another person. It defines surrender as no longer resisting an enemy or opponent, but instead, submitting to their authority. This is actually a suitable definition for how we are to submit, or surrender, to our Lord and Savior, Jesus Christ. We no longer view God as our adversary; we stop viewing Him as our opponent, and we surrender. He is God, who is above all else. We give all honor, glory, and praise to

God. He is the ultimate authority in our lives. He is who we will give an account to at the final judgement. We must submit ourselves to God.

Submitting to God requires us to place ourselves under God's authority and protection. Jeremiah 29:11 says, "For I know the thoughts that I think toward you, saith the Lord, thoughts of peace, and not of evil, to give you an expected end." We must give God all authority in our lives. He must have the first and final say.

When we sin against God, we are choosing to remove ourselves from under His umbrella of authority and protection. In order to maintain our position under His merciful umbrella of authority, we must come into agreement with what God says through His Word, and through the prompting of His Holy Spirit.

Romans 6:13 tells us, "Neither yield ye your members as instruments of unrighteousness unto sin: but yield yourselves unto God, as those that are alive from the dead, and your members as instruments of righteousness unto God." We must submit ourselves entirely to God, not obeying our flesh, or man, but obeying God alone.

Submitting to God involves surrendering our will for His. Proverbs 14:12 tells us, "There is a way which seemeth right unto a man, but the end thereof are the ways of death." We must recognize that we will never know better than Almighty God. His plans and purpose for us are perfect and righteous. Seeking His will for our lives means getting out of the way, and letting Him do what only He can do.

All that we plan for ourselves, all that we think best for ourselves, and the path that we think is right, must be surrendered to God. We must surrender all to Christ. His plan, path, and purpose must replace the plans, path, and purpose, that we desire and designed. James 4:7 says, "Submit yourselves therefore to God." The only way to truly obey the Lord is to submit our will in exchange for God's will for our lives.

We must submit, or surrender, our minds to God. Philippians 2:5 says, "Let this mind be in you, which was also in Christ Jesus." Our minds produce ungodliness, and our thoughts are wicked, apart from God's transforming power. When we fully submit our minds, our thoughts, to God, the Holy Spirit takes hold of our thinking. 2 Corinthians 10:5 says, "Casting down imaginations, and every high thing that exalteth itself against the knowledge of God, and bringing into captivity every thought to the obedience of Christ;" Committing our minds, our thoughts, to His authority is the way to victory over our minds. We must let God filter our thoughts, and purify our minds.

When we submit our lives fully to Christ, we will begin to experience true freedom. God wants complete dominion over our hearts, minds, and bodies. Romans 12:1-2 tells us, "I beseech you therefore, brethren, by the mercies of God, that ye present your bodies a living sacrifice, holy, acceptable unto God, which is your reasonable service. And be not conformed to this world: but be ye transformed by the renewing of your mind, that ye may prove what is that good, and acceptable, and perfect, will of God." Yes, not only our minds, but also our bodies.

It is not up to us to decide what we do with our bodies. Our bodies belong to the Lord as well. Hebrews 10:12 tells us, "Let us draw near with a true heart in full assurance of faith, having our hearts sprinkled from an evil conscience, and our bodies washed with pure water." Surrender all. Submit all.

The Lord is not interested in being Lord of only portions of our lives. He wants to be Lord of our entire lives. He will not share authority over our lives with anyone or anything, not even us. We must fully commit to submit all areas of our lives to Our Lord and Savior, Jesus Christ.

~Brokenness

Brokenness before God begins when we are authentically torn to pieces over our sin. It is when we know that there is only one, Jesus Christ, who is capable of purifying our hearts. Brokenness before God is necessary in order to experience the fullness of Christ in our lives.

Our Lord and Savior, Jesus Christ sees our brokenness, and uses it for His glory. He sees our brokenness as us desiring nothing more than Jesus. He sees our brokenness as us being truly repentant over our sin. Brokenness is a condition of the heart. Brokenness is humility. When we are broken before God, we abdicate the throne of our lives, and allow our Lord and Savior, Jesus Christ, His rightful place in our lives. Brokenness before God is a choice.

Brokenness does not equate to a pretentiously sorrowful, or dramatically downward disposition. Brokenness is not a feeling, but a response to the grace and mercy extended to us from God. Brokenness is an attribute of a believer that God requires. It is not something that indicates weakness. Brokenness is complete surrender to Jesus, depending on only Him, and believing God for everything. It is a condition of humility toward God. It is a realization that we are sinners saved by grace, and an attitude of overwhelming gratefulness.

It is the belief in who Christ says He is, and who we are in Christ.

Brokenness before God is truly living in the acknowledgement that we can do nothing, and we are nothing, apart from God. It is a state of surrender and obedience to Almighty God. Being broken before God is when the only one whose opinion matters to us is The Lord's. Being broken before God, is when everything in and of ourselves is dead, and all that can be seen is Jesus. Brokenness is what God desires for us.

Brokenness is achieved when the walls of pride, arrogance, self-sufficiency, self-centeredness, stubbornness, independence, and sin are shattered, and completely obliterated. Yes, in order for brokenness before Almighty God can take place, we must recognize that we are absolutely nothing without Him. Psalm 34:18 says, "The LORD is nigh unto them that are of a broken heart; and saveth such as be of a contrite spirit." Our sin must break our hearts, just as it breaks God's heart. God desires to use us, fully repentant for our sin, for His glory.

We must be broken before God, fully repentant for our past sins, current sins, and future sins. Brokenness is the ability to come before God, swiftly, with a repentant spirit, over our sin. True brokenness is when our sin causes true repentance.

True repentance generates transformation. We turn from our sin, to return to it no more. Our acknowledgment of our sin breaks us. We desire nothing more than to have our relationship with our Lord and Savior restored. Brokenness is necessary to truly see the manifestation of Christ in our lives.

In order to be broken, we must believe that our hearts are desperately wicked, and in need of Jesus. We must seek God's will, not our own, in every moment of our lives. When we humbly welcome the Lord to search our hearts and cleanse us from all unrighteousness, we are broken.

Psalm 139:23-24 says, "Search me, O God, and know my heart: try me, and know my thoughts: And see if there be any wicked way in me, and lead me in the way everlasting." When our sin breaks our hearts, we are quick to confess it, and then promptly ask for forgiveness; this is when we are broken. I John 1:9 says, "If we confess our sins, he is faithful and just to forgive us our sins, and to cleanse us from all unrighteousness." We must desire brokenness.

James 4:6 tells us, "But he giveth more grace. Wherefore he saith, God resisteth the proud, but giveth grace unto the humble." God wants us to be completely emptied of ourselves. Our pride and selfishness must go in order for us to be broken before God. A lifestyle of humility and sacrifice to God is what He expects. We can have joy in our brokenness, because we are relying on the Holy Spirit of God for all things. Psalms 51:17 says, "The sacrifices of God are a broken spirit: a broken and a contrite heart, O God, thou wilt not despise." There is peace, joy, and beauty, in our brokenness.

~Christ's Ambassadors

Our United States Government defines an ambassador as the President's highest-ranking representative to a specific nation. To be effective, the ambassador must have strong leadership qualities, be a good manager, be a resilient negotiator, and be well respected.

An earthly ambassador represents and imparts the desires and intentions of the government from where he or she originates. Being an ambassador for nations here on earth has only temporary significance. If an earthly ambassador is esteemed so greatly, just think about how prestigious our calling is, as ambassadors for the King of Kings, Almighty God.

The moment we surrender our lives to Jesus Christ, we renounce our citizenship in this world. We voluntarily relinquished our earthly citizenship, for citizenship in the Kingdom of God. When we accept Jesus' free gift of salvation, through placing our faith and trust in Him, we are instantly naturalized into God's Kingdom.

Our citizenship is now found in heaven, through Jesus Christ. Ephesians 2:19 puts it this way, "Now therefore ye are no more strangers and foreigners, but fellow citizens with the saints, and of the household of God;" Take a moment and really absorb the magnitude of responsibility, privilege, and honor that your new citizenship entails.

Our position as ambassadors representing Jesus Christ carries a far weightier significance than any other calling. Our calling has eternal significance. In Ephesians 6:20 Paul writes, "For which I am an ambassador in bonds: that therein I may speak boldly, as I ought to speak."

Paul was representing Christ while a prisoner. We represent Christ without any constraints. We represent Christ in complete freedom. To be effective, we must hold firmly to the truth of God's Word, and live our lives to honor and please God.

Our responsibility is to represent well the intentions, desires, and will of Jesus Christ to everyone that God gives us the opportunity to interact with. We, like Paul, must share the love of Jesus boldly and without any reservation. Paul says in Romans 1:16, "For I am not ashamed of the gospel of Christ: for it is the power of God unto salvation to everyone that believeth." Let's ask God to impart to us a mindset as Paul had.

We are ambassadors, representing the King of Kings and Lord of Lords: Jesus Christ. As Christ's ambassadors, how are we representing Christ's character and love? For some of those with whom our paths intersect, we may be the only avenue through which they are given the opportunity to see Christ on this side of heaven. We must honor Christ in word and deed, without exception, at all times.

What an honor and a privilege we have been extended, in Jesus' name. II Corinthians 5:20 says, "Now then we are ambassadors for Christ, as though God did beseech you by us: we pray you in Christ's stead, be ye reconciled to God." God has empowered us to live our lives in alignment with His will, to hold true to every word written in the Bible, and to love as He loves.

Let's honor God with every aspect of our lives. The world has no hold on us; it has nothing to offer us. Christ paid a handsome price for our freedom from the bondage of the world and our flesh. Give the enemy of our souls no opportunity to cause blemish or stain to our testimony, as we represent Christ as His ambassadors.

He sent His Holy Spirit to dwell in us. Therefore, let us represent He who is in us, well. I Peter 3:15 tells us, "But sanctify the Lord God in your hearts: and be ready always to give an answer to every man that asketh you a reason of the hope that is in you with meekness and fear:" I am thankful, and greatly humbled by the commission to act as His ambassador, to bring glory and honor to His Great Name. God has appointed us as representatives, for His glory. Let's represent Him well, because He is worthy.

~Please God, Not Men

We live in a culture where we are encouraged to promote and edify self. We are persuaded to do whatever it takes to gain ever increasing popularity, and to give our egos a boost. We have all been there. As Christ followers, we must remember who it is we represent. We must keep in mind that God discourages seeking the approval of man over the approval of the One who saved our souls.

It is very easy to fall into the trap of seeking affirmation from people instead of God. It is not God's will for us to seek and secure an audience of men to affirm, validate, or approve of who we are. We do not need man's approval of what we have to offer.

The only one from whom we should seek affirmation and approval is God. Matthew 5:6 says, "Blessed are they which do hunger and thirst after righteousness: for they shall be filled." Our goal should never be to impress men. Only God, not people, can fulfill all of our needs.

Our pride and ego tend to inch their way to the podium of our lives, in order to gain the attention and approval of men. If God has blessed you with a platform, or a position of influence, use it as though you have an audience of one. I Thessalonians 2:4 says, "But as we were allowed of God to be put in trust with the gospel, even so we speak; not as pleasing men, but God, which trieth our hearts." We are not called to win favor and popularity with people. We are called to bring glory to God, and to please Him only.

We must check our motivation for everything we do and say, making certain that we are edifying The Lord. Our responsibility is to check our motives to ensure that we are not focused on improving our image or status in the eyes of people. Paul was being accused by the Judaizers of being a man pleaser.

Paul is qualifying his motives, to show that they are in alignment with God, in Galatians 1:10-12. He writes, "For do I now persuade men, or God? or do I seek to please men? For if I yet pleased men, I should not be the servant of Christ. But I certify you, brethren, that the gospel which was preached of me is not after man. For I neither received it of man, neither was I taught it, but by the revelation of Jesus Christ." We should use these verses to check our purpose and motives as well. If we are seeking the approval of men, and not advancing the pure unadulterated gospel, we are failing to put God in His rightful place.

When our hearts and minds are stayed on The Lord, and we are seeking His will in all we do, we are less likely to be self-serving people pleasers. If we are misplacing our focus, and placing it on what people think of us, over what God thinks of us, we will be of little service to The Kingdom of God. Our heart's posture must be fixed on seeking God's good pleasure, and the best interest of all who are involved. If God gives you a platform of any kind, it comes with great responsibility.

John 12:43 says, "For they loved the praise of men more than the praise of God." Our goal in life should never be to gain the praise of men. The love that God has for us, and the favor that He has showered upon us, through Christ's shed blood, is more than enough.

I Corinthians 10:31 says, "Whether therefore ye eat, or drink, or whatsoever ye do, do all to the glory of God." Keeping this verse as our key motivation for all that we do and say, is crucial. The last thing we want is to be ineffective for The Lord. Our objectives must always line up with God's objective, which is to spread the gospel, and bring glory and honor to our Lord and Savior, Jesus Christ.

Romans 12:3 warns of keeping ourselves free of self-adoration and praise. It reads, "For I say, through the grace given unto me, to every man that is among you, not to think of himself more highly than he ought to think; but to think soberly, according as God hath dealt to every man the measure of faith." When we seek the praise and affirmation of men, it puffs up our ego, and causes us to think too highly of ourselves. Leave it to God to shower us with His affirmation and approval, which is pure and Holy. There is no other approval that we should want or need.

We must give Jesus praise and honor, and keep our focus on the Lord. Praise Him for all that He does in and through you. Keep your objectives clear at all times. Our objective should always be to please the Lord in all we do.

~When God Gives You An Assignment

Consider the assignments that God had given some Biblical giants. Consider the assignment God has assigned to each of us.

Isaiah 43 :7 tells us, "Even every one that is called by my name: for I have created him for my glory, I have formed him; yea, I have made him." God created us with the main purpose of glorifying God. Our purpose was never intended to glorify self. Our main assignment is, and always has been, to bring glory to God. John 15:8 shows us our purpose when it says, "Herein is my Father glorified, that ye bear much fruit; so shall ye be my disciples."

Our purpose, is to reflect Christ in all that we are and do. Every son and daughter of the King of Kings has an individual assignment, to carry out our purpose. When God speaks to you about your assignment, through the encouragement and persistent prompting from His Holy Spirit, we must obediently respond with, "yes." Through our assignment, we are able to fulfill our purpose of bringing glory to Almighty God.

We will look at a few Biblical Giants, and their specific assignments.

Moses:

Moses had a single assignment. He was to bring God's people, the Israelites, out of Egypt.

Exodus 3:10 says, "Come now therefore, and I will send thee unto Pharaoh, that thou mayest bring forth my people the children of Israel out of Egypt."

Joshua:

Joshua's assignment was to lead the Israelites into the Promised Land, to take possession of it.

In Joshua 1:2, The Lord spoke to Joshua. He said, "Moses my servant is dead; now therefore arise, go over this Jordan, thou, and all this people, unto the land which I do give to them, even to the children of Israel."

Jonah:

Go to Nineveh and warn them of God's wrath that would arise if they fail to repent.

Jonah 1:1-2 - "Now the word of the Lord came unto Jonah the son of Amittai, saying, Arise, go to Nineveh, that great city, and cry against it; for their wickedness is come up before me."

Solomon:

Solomon's assignment was to build the temple.
1 Kings 6:14: "So Solomon built the house, and finished it."

Mary:

Fulfill the virgin birth of Jesus
Luke 1:29-31: "And the angel said unto her, Fear not, Mary: for thou hast found favor with God. And, behold, thou shalt conceive in thy womb, and bring forth a son, and shalt call his name Jesus."

Paul:

Paul's assignment was to spread the Good News of Jesus Christ to the Gentiles.

Acts 9:15: "But the Lord said unto him, Go thy way: for he is a chosen vessel unto me, to bear my name before the Gentiles, and kings, and the children of Israel."

Take some time to look up the assignments of other men and women in the Bible.

You can be sure that anything done with selfish ambition, is not an assignment from God. John 17:4 reads, "I have glorified thee on the earth: I have finished the work which thou gavest me to do." It is still all about Jesus, and representing Him, not ourselves. God doesn't intend for us to be overwhelmed with multiple assignments. Our ultimate assignment is to bring glory and honor to God.

He is a God of purpose. God has a plan and purpose for each of us. The Holy Spirit will designate an assignment for each of us to accomplish, but we must have our hearts and minds stayed on Christ, to hear from Him. Our assignments are given for God's glory, not ours. The assignments that God gives us may be one for a lifetime, or He may assign different assignments according to our different seasons of life.

For me personally, God spoke to me before my husband and I began having children. The Holy Spirit made it very clear that my assignment would be to end my career, and devote myself to raising our children in The Lord. He also said within this assignment, that His desire for me was to provide all of their education through the completion of high school. He wanted us to establish a firm foundation for our children, rooted in Jesus. In complete acceptance of my assignment, I did exactly that.

God plucked me out of my life as I knew it, and I stayed home with my three precious children for 20 years. He showed me clearly that this was my exclusive assignment. I loved every moment of this assignment. One of the most rewarding, challenging, and cherished gifts ever given to me, was staying home to raise and educate our children.

God gave me a short period of what felt like barrenness before He spoke to me about my next assignment. My current assignment, which was clearly given to me from God, is not only writing, but also advocating for those who are victims of human trafficking and addiction. I am grateful that God gives me the words to write each day, as well as the opportunity to help women who need authentic love, and encouragement.

What assignment has God outlined for you? Remember, the assignment that He gives to each of us, is for His glory. Are you listening to His voice? Colossians 3:23-24 implores us, "And whatsoever ye do, do it heartily, as to the Lord, and not unto men; Knowing that of the Lord ye shall receive the reward of the inheritance: for ye serve the Lord Christ." We all have an assignment placed upon us by God.

Have you taken hold of the opportunity to play your part in God's perfect plan? Psalm 32:8 says, "I will instruct thee and teach thee in the way which thou shalt go: I will guide thee with mine eye." We must Keep our hearts and minds focused on The Lord, so we don't miss an opportunity. With a clean heart Isaiah heard his assignment from God, and replied, "Then I heard the voice of the Lord, saying, "Whom shall I send, and who will go for Us?" Then I said, "Here am I. Send me!" Are you ready for your assignment?

~Discernment

Godly discernment is critical for our spiritual strength and growth.

We are faced with one decision after another, all day, every day. We are not naturally equipped to consistently make the right decisions, without the Spirit of the living God working in and through us. We battle with right and wrong, because of our sin nature. It is only because of Jesus that we can filter through right and wrong; wise and unwise; moral and immoral; and so on.

It is because of the wisdom and discernment given to us by God, that we are able to walk in full alignment with His will for our lives. Hebrews 5:14 says, "But strong meat belongeth to them that are of full age, even those who by reason of use have their senses exercised to discern both good and evil." Some of us lack the power and ability to choose rightly simply because we have not given all authority and control over every aspect of our lives to Christ. We lack discernment when we fail to yield to the Spirit of God in each decision we must make.

Discernment is the ability to know the difference between good and bad. Discernment is the ability to know the difference between what is beneficial, and what is detrimental. Discernment is the ability to know what is profitable, and what is unprofitable. Discernment is the ability to say no when needed. Discernment is the ability to know the difference between fruitful living, and an unfruitful existence.

Discernment is the ability to know if a word is from God, or not. Having Godly discernment empowers, equips, and aligns us with the Word of God, and His will for our lives. Finally, discernment is a nonnegotiable for all those who have placed their faith and trust in our Lord and Savior, Jesus Christ.

To be able to discern, or understand, the things of God, you must have the spirit of God dwelling within your heart. He clears up the fog of unbelief that our flesh, the devil, and the ideas of the world, have planted in our hearts and minds. I Corinthians 2: 14 says, "But the natural man receiveth not the things of the Spirit of God: for they are foolishness unto him: neither can he know them, because they are spiritually discerned." This explains why unbelievers are unable to know the difference between Godly choices and ungodly choices.

All things concerning the Lord are spiritually discerned. Godly discernment is the ability to know the difference between truth and falsehood. It is through our relationship with, dependence on, and obedience to Christ, that we are clothed with a discerning spirit.

It is our personal responsibility to honor God in our lives. It is then that we are able to activate this powerful gift of discernment. Colossians 2: 8 says, "Beware lest any man spoil you through philosophy and vain deceit, after the tradition of men, after the rudiments of the world, and not after Christ."

It is because of the gift of discernment that we are able to distinguish the truth of God from the ever so subtle, and oftentimes blatant, lies of the enemy of our souls. I Thessalonians 5:21 tells us, "Prove all things; hold fast that which is good." We must run everything through a spiritual filter, the Word of God, and cling to that which is good, and reprove all that is out of alignment with the Word of God.

To possess a spirit of discernment, we must surrender our will for God's will. Our desires, must be His desires. Allowing God to equip us with a spirit of Godly discernment, is key to making wise, sound, and biblical decisions in all areas of our lives. Utilizing Godly discernment keeps us out of compromising situations, and empowers us to live a God honoring, and sanctified life.

If you lack Godly discernment, get in alignment with God. Consider God first, in all decision making. Get in the Word daily, study, pray for the Spirit of discernment, and let your lifestyle reflect Jesus. Philippians 2:5 says, "Let this mind be in you, which was also in Christ Jesus:" We must stop obeying our flesh, and walk in obedience with the Lord. The spirit of discernment is ours, if we have placed our faith and trust in Jesus. Claim it, and actively use it.

~False Teachers

There are many people in the world who preach and teach false information, and call it truth. It is imperative that we refrain from placing merit in something, merely because it sounds good. We must examine the spirit behind what we are hearing. Is it coming from a place of biblical truth, or is it tainted with false teaching?

People can be sincere, but sincerely wrong. Deceptive spirits tend to mix a little truth with a lot of lies, or they sprinkle a lie within a lot of truth. This is why we must know, and believe, the Word of God. We will then be equipped to test everything against scripture.

I John 4:1- 3 says, "Beloved, believe not every spirit, but try the spirits whether they are of God: because many false prophets are gone out into the world. Hereby know ye the Spirit of God: Every spirit that confesseth that Jesus Christ is come in the flesh is of God: And every spirit that confesseth not that Jesus Christ is come in the flesh is not of God: and this is that spirit of antichrist, whereof ye have heard that it should come; and even now already is it in the world."

In today's culture, there is a very popular idea, that not everything in God's Word applies to us today. There is the idea that we can bend and twist the Word of God, to align with our own version of truth. This is a lie from the pit of Hell.

We must not manipulate or dismiss any part of the Bible. Every Word of the Bible is truth, useful, to be applied to our lives, and it delivers truth for better understanding of who God is.

II Timothy 3:16-17 says, "All scripture is given by inspiration of God, and is profitable for doctrine, for reproof, for correction, for instruction in righteousness: That the man of God may be perfect, thoroughly furnished unto all good works." Even the Old Testament is useful to help us understand God's character, will, and plan.

The Word of God must not be altered, nor can it be transformed to align with ever changing and worldly ways of sinful man. Everything that we hear, everything that is being presented to us as truth, must align with the will of God, which is outlined in scripture. If what we are hearing does not point to Jesus, who came in the flesh to dwell among us, died, and rose again; then steer clear of the messenger. This is the ultimate litmus test.

The Holy Spirit will make us aware of false teaching, if we are walking in synch with the Lord, and if we know the Word. II Timothy 4: 3-4 warns us, "For the time will come when they will not endure sound doctrine; but after their own lusts shall they heap to themselves teachers, having itching ears; And they shall turn away their ears from the truth, and shall be turned unto fables." We must be very cautious when adopting someone's message as truth. Test everything, to be certain that it is Truth. Truth is the Word of God, and truth is Jesus. If Jesus isn't being magnified, if Jesus isn't being glorified, then turn and flee.

We must not lend an ear to any messenger who alters the Truth of God's word to align with an ungodly agenda, cultural trends, or ungodly practices. Cling to Truth. Cling to Jesus. John 17:17 tells us, "Sanctify them through thy truth:

thy word is truth." We must know God's Word, and fervently pray that God will give us the gift of discernment. If it is not in full alignment with the Word of God, do not subscribe to it at all.

~Pride

An attitude of pride, keeps us alienated from God. Pride interferes with God's plan and purpose for our lives.

Pride is contrary to God, and His desire for us. Pride is an overestimation of self. Pride is an inclination toward autonomy. Pride is when we say not your will God, but mine be done. Pride is an attitude of arrogance. Pride is when we see no need to look to God to sustain us, but instead we look to self. Pride creates the idea within, to depend on no one but ourselves. Pride says we can decide for ourselves what is good, and what isn't.

In the Old Testament, we learn about the nation of Edom, who was cruel to Israel, and very prideful. Obadiah prophesied against the arrogance of Edom. Obadiah 1:3 says, "The pride of thine heart hath deceived thee, thou that dwellest in the clefts of the rock, whose habitation is high; that saith in his heart, who shall bring me down to the ground?" Pride displays overconfidence in self.

The spirit of pride does not originate from God, nor is it endorsed by God. Proverbs 8:13 says, "The fear of the Lord is to hate evil: pride, and arrogance, and the evil way, and the froward mouth, do I hate." God abhors pride. God resists the proud, but gives grace to the humble. I Peter 5:5-6 says, "Likewise, ye younger, submit yourselves unto the elder. Yea, all of you be subject one to another, and be clothed with humility: for God resisteth the proud, and giveth grace to the humble. Humble yourselves therefore under the mighty hand of God, that he may exalt you in due time."

God delights in those who are clothed in humility. He does not exalt a prideful person. Isaiah 13:11 says, "And I will punish the world for their evil, and the wicked for their iniquity; and I will cause the arrogance of the proud to cease, and will lay low the haughtiness of the terrible." God wants us to forsake the spirit of pride. Pride does not come from God.

It is because of pride that mankind does not seek God. Pride creates a barrier between us and God. It is because of pride, that we become stubborn and arrogant toward others and God. We are called to be humble in spirit, which is the direct opposite of pride. Psalm 10:4 "The wicked, through the pride of his countenance, will not seek after God: God is not in all his thoughts."

Pride is a tool that the devil uses to blind us to our need for Jesus. We get consumed by pride, and think that we are self-sufficient and that we do not need a Savior. Pride causes us to believe the lie that we have it all figured out, and we are just fine. Pride prevents us from admitting that we are wrong. Pride causes division among people. It is the spirit of Pride that is at the core of sin. Pride is a misaligned heart posture toward God.

We must come into an agreement with God, that pride is evil and disgraceful. Furthermore, no good thing results from a spirit of pride. In Mark 7: 20-23, Jesus is addressing His disciples when He says, "And he said, That which cometh out of the man, that defileth the man. For from within, out of the heart of men, proceed evil thoughts, adulteries, fornications, murders, thefts, covetousness, wickedness, deceit, lasciviousness, an evil eye, blasphemy, pride, foolishness: All these evil things come from within, and defile the man."

Pride originated with the devil desiring to be like God. The devil had an inflated view of self, and as a result, got exiled from heaven. Pride says that we know better than God. Pride was behind Adam and Eve's decision in the Garden. Pride is from the devil, and a worldly badge of honor.

I John 2:16 tells us, "For all that is in the world, the lust of the flesh, and the lust of the eyes, and the pride of life, is not of the Father, but is of the world." We must decide to cling to godliness, and truth. Choose to stay grounded, with your feet planted, with a humble spirit, in the Word, which is truth.

Choose humility over pride. Proverbs 29:23 says "A man's pride shall bring him low: but honour shall uphold the humble in spirit." Choosing pride, is choosing death. Follow in Christ's footsteps, and walk in the spirit, with humility. Proverbs 16:18-19 tells us, "Pride goeth before destruction, and an haughty spirit before a fall. Better it is to be of a humble spirit with the lowly, than to divide the spoil with the proud."

Wisdom and understanding come from our Lord and Savior, Jesus Christ. If we are led by the Spirit of God, we will not give way to pride. Proverbs 14:3 says, "In the mouth of the foolish is a rod of pride: but the lips of the wise shall preserve them." Choose humility.

~Humility

Pride is not an attribute, or character trait, that Christ wants for us. We are instructed to be clothed in humility. Obedience through humility is ultimately what God desires from each of us.

Humility is achieved when we display a modest, or low estimation of self. We are humble in spirit if we are considerate, compassionate, and possess a spirit of selflessness. Humility is what God commands of all His children. I Peter 5:5 tells us, "be clothed with humility: for God resisteth the proud, and giveth grace to the humble."

If we are humble, we are not proud. If we are humble, we are not arrogant. If we are humble, we are not haughty. If we are humble, we do not have a superior attitude. If we are humble, we are not pretentious. If we are humble, we are not flamboyant. If we are humble, we are not boastful. If we are humble, we are not egotistical. Qualities of someone who is clothed in humility include: meekness, unassertive, modest, unpretentious, and self-effacing.

It is with a spirit of humility that we put others before ourselves. When we truly place the needs of others above our own needs, we have an understanding of humility. Philippians 2:3-4 says, "Let nothing be done through strife or vainglory; but in lowliness of mind let each esteem other

better than themselves. Look not every man on his own
things, but every man also on the things of others." When we
are humble at heart, we no longer have a high estimation of
ourselves. We do not think of ourselves more highly than we
should. Those who are truly clothed in humility, will always
look for ways to bless, serve, and encourage others.

It is with a spirit of humility, that God will raise us up.
James 4:2 says, "Humble yourselves in the sight of the Lord,
and he shall lift you up." The only way the Lord will raise us
up is if we display humility before Him. When we are humble
before God, we truly trust Him to provide for us, and we are
patient with God. We understand that God desires His best
for us, and we accept that things do not always go the way
that we intend for them to go. When we manifest humility,
and do not try to exalt ourselves, God will elevate us in His
time.

We must be dependent on God, and wait on Him. I Peter
5:6 also states, "Humble yourselves therefore under the
mighty hand of God, that he may exalt you in due time."

It is with a spirit of humility that God will use us to bring
glory to His name. Matthew 6:2 says, "Therefore when thou
doest thine alms, do not sound a trumpet before thee, as the
hypocrites do in the synagogues and in the streets, that they
may have glory of men. Verily I say unto you, They have their
reward." When God chooses to use us, we must not be proud,
and desire attention and accolades for how we have been used
to glorify God.

It is because of the grace of God, and His power, that we
are able to do or accomplish anything at all. We must put on
humility, and resist attention seeking. John 3:30 tells us, "He
must increase, but I must decrease." This is in direct
opposition to our fleshly desire to achieve notoriety and fame
for the things that we do and accomplish. Proverbs 22:4 says,

"By humility and the fear of the LORD are riches, and honor, and life." Be still, and be used of God.

Ephesians 3:20-21 says, "Now unto him that is able to do exceeding abundantly above all that we ask or think, according to the power that worketh in us, Unto him be glory in the church by Christ Jesus throughout all ages, world without end. Amen."

~Changed

When we surrender our all to the authority and will of Jesus Christ, everything must become new. If we desire true freedom in Christ, everything must change. II Corinthians 5:17 tells us, "Therefore if any man be in Christ, he is a new creature: old things are passed away; behold, all things are become new."

Too often, so called Christians are behaving nothing like redeemed children of the King of Kings. This simply should not be. It is contradictory to claim to be a Christ follower and continue to live in disobedience to the Word of God. It is time to yield to the Holy Spirit of God in our lives, and through obedience, take on the mind of Christ.

Romans 12:2 says, "And be not conformed to this world: but be ye transformed by the renewing of your mind, that ye may prove what [is] that good, and acceptable, and perfect, will of God." It is not impossible to obey the Lord in all things. Quit giving so much power to the flesh. It is time for change. Say no to your flesh. It is time for change.

Our way of thinking, how we spend our time, with whom we spend our time, and who and what we allow to influence us, must change. There must be no exceptions. Do not believe the lie that one drink is ok, or weed is almost legal so it is fine.

Do not adjust your standards to accommodate your flesh. God's standards for righteousness are high.

Yes, all forms of sexual contact outside of marriage between a man and woman is sin. Yes, consuming media filled with immorality, violence, and the like, grieves the Lord. We cannot continue to live any way we want, and expect God to bless our lives. We can no longer live in sin, yet expect to experience freedom. We are called to greatness. We have been granted power and position in Christ Jesus, but we are rendered ineffective when we yield to our flesh, instead of the Holy Spirit. It is time for change.

One of the most difficult adjustments that is necessary, is abandoning unhealthy and unfruitful behaviors and relationships from our past. Additionally, we must align our lives with the Word of God, not the world or our flesh. Light and darkness have nothing in common. II Corinthians 6:14 says, "Be ye not unequally yoked together with unbelievers: for what fellowship hath righteousness with unrighteousness? and what communion hath light with darkness?"

It is important to obey the Lord in all things. To ignore His commands is prideful as well as an indication that we are not willing to surrender our entire lives to Jesus. We are going to struggle unnecessarily, guaranteed, if we fail to live our lives in obedience to the Lord. It is time for change.

It is unwise to think that we can maintain our relationship with the world and hang with friends that are in the world, and stay in alignment with the will of the Lord. To be free, is to no longer be bound to the world or worldly things and ideas. To be free, is to no longer fulfill the desires of our flesh. James 4:4 says, "Ye adulterers and adulteresses, know ye not that the friendship of the world is enmity with God? whosoever therefore will be a friend of the world is the enemy of God." We must surround ourselves with godly influences, activities, and habits.

In order to strengthen and solidify our faith, we must cultivate our relationship with the Lord, and those who diligently seek the heart of God. Proverbs 27:17 says, "Iron sharpeneth iron; so a man sharpeneth the countenance of his friend." Those who do not love the Lord are incapable of coming alongside us, and encouraging us in our walk with the Lord.

Spending time wallowing in, or even wetting our toes in our previous sinful environment, and engaging in the activities of our past, is not only a very bad idea, but also extremely dangerous. We risk falling away, and it just isn't worth it. We must treasure our new life in Christ, and forsake all things unrighteous. Some say these ideas I propose are legalistic, and I say they are biblical.

Those who cry legalism want an excuse to keep sinning. Those who cry, "but there is no condemnation," need to reread those verses in context. They are not referring to excusing sin. We must rid ourselves of pride and stubbornness, and long for the things of God. The enemy will tempt us, try to entice us, and even lure us back into the life we died to. It is time for change.

We are given all we require to resist the devil when we placed our faith and trust in Christ. Proverbs 13:20 tells us, "He that walketh with wise men shall be wise: but a companion of fools shall be destroyed." I will boldly say, that all forms and levels of ungodliness must cease.

The drinking, smoking, cursing, sex outside of marriage, unwholesome talk, lewd television, perversion, and anything else that we know displeases our Lord and Savior, Jesus Christ, must stop. It is that simple, and it is not legalistic to demand it. Godly standards are the only standards that we should desire. It is time for change.

We must bury our old selves, along with all soul ties and worldly activities and associations that previously influenced our lives. Romans 6:4 says, "Therefore we are buried with him by baptism into death: that like as Christ was raised up from the dead by the glory of the Father, even so we also should walk in newness of life." Christians who convince themselves that they can live double lives are deceiving themselves.

Galatians 6:7 says, "Be not deceived; God is not mocked: for whatsoever a man soweth, that shall he also reap." We must stop trying to justify our sin, choose Christ and His ways, and be blessed. It is time for change.

It is true that we all struggle with sin, because of our sin nature. We cannot use this as an excuse to continue to blatantly sin against God. We must choose Christ over all. With the Holy Spirit of God dwelling in us, He gives us power and authority over any sin that attempts to seep into our lives. It is time for change.

~Captured But Free

Freedom is a condition of not being controlled, imprisoned, or enslaved. Freedom is declared, sought after, and dreamed about, but true freedom is only found through surrendering our lives over to our Lord and Savior, Jesus Christ. We all, in our flesh, desire freedom to live as we choose, speak without hindrances, think independently, make our own choices, and create our own destiny. What do we gain from these freedoms, other than temporary satisfaction and pleasure? True freedom that is eternal is only found when we surrender our all to Jesus Christ.

It sounds ironic I know: to surrender our all, in order to be truly free. The truth is that without Christ at the center of our lives, we are slaves to our flesh, sin, the world, and the devil. It is when we are walking in the Spirit of the Lord, that we are free.

II Corinthians 3:17 says, "Now the Lord is that Spirit: and where the Spirit of the Lord is, there is liberty." We all desperately need to be captured by God's love, saving grace, and mercy. We all have gone astray, and have wondered in the wilderness of our sin, rebellion, and shame. There must be a point when we stop running from the pursuit of The Holy Spirit of God, and allow Him to truly capture us.

When our hearts, minds, and souls are captured by Christ, and we give Him complete authority over our entire lives, this is freedom. We are set free from the stronghold of sin, and the power sin has over us when we are captured by Christ.

Until we are captured, we walk in darkness, and we are clothed in unrighteousness. This is how it is for every one of us up until we surrender our will, for the will of our Lord and Savior, Jesus Christ. Romans 6:18 says, "Being then made free from sin, ye became the servants of righteousness." When we are captured by Christ, we walk in the light, and we are instantly clothed in righteousness. Who wouldn't want to be captured, but free?

God, through the shed blood of Jesus Christ, has laid out a perfect plan to capture the hearts and minds of all mankind. Because we are born with a sin nature, and God created us with free will, we choose to sin. This choice, separates us from Almighty God. We are imprisoned by our sin, and its consequences.

Galatians 5:1 tells us, "Stand fast therefore in the liberty wherewith Christ hath made us free, and be not entangled again with the yoke of bondage." We must choose to be captured by the Lord, only to be set free from the bondage and from the penalty of our sin.

The penalty of sin is spiritual death and eternal separation from God. Romans 6:23 says, "For the wages of sin is death; but the gift of God is eternal life through Jesus Christ our Lord." But, Glory to God, if we allow God to capture us, and we repent and turn from our sin, we will be free from the penalty of our sin. John 8:36 assures us, "If the Son therefore shall make you free, ye shall be free indeed." Choose freedom, and sin no more.

Be captured by Jesus. The result of being captured by Jesus, is freedom from the penalty of your sin.

~Freedom

Freedom is one of the greatest advantages of salvation, next to being absolved from the penalty of our sin, and the promise of eternity in the presence of the Lord. Freedom from the law, and freedom from the bondage of sin is priceless.

When we were under the law, there was no power in the law to save. When we were bound by our sin and shame; we were slaves to sin. Then came Jesus, to rescue us, and grant us freedom. Jesus is the sinless lamb of God, who came to earth to die in our place. He came to set us free from the law, and the power of sin and death.

This freedom is available to all who place their faith and trust in our Lord and Savior, Jesus Christ. John 8: 36 says, "If the Son therefore shall make you free, ye shall be free indeed." Jesus went to the cross with purpose, and that purpose was to free us from the law, as well as the grip of sin.

Being under the law, and all of the rules within the law, provided no salvation. The law only made us aware of our sin. I John 3:4 says, "Whosoever committeth sin transgresseth also the law: for sin is the transgression of the law." The law had no power to save us from sin's penalty, which is death. The blood of Jesus is the only way to freedom. John 1:17 tells us, ""For the law was given by Moses, but grace and truth came by Jesus Christ."

The Old Testament law pointed to the coming of Jesus. Romans 10:4 reads, "For Christ is the end of the law for righteousness to everyone that believeth." The law was no longer the perceived means to righteousness, and eternity in the presence of Almighty God. Jesus Christ fulfilled the law, and acceptance of Jesus is the only pathway to God. We obey Jesus, not the law. Freedom from the law is found in obedience to Jesus. Galatians 5:13 says, "For, brethren, ye have been called unto liberty; only use not liberty for an occasion to the flesh, but by love serve one another."

Freedom is experienced when we no longer are bound by sin, and we freely live to honor and please God. This is freedom, to unashamedly worship and obey our Lord and Savior, Jesus Christ. We no longer need to be in bondage to sin. Sin should no longer be our master, and we should no longer give way to its seduction.

Some Christ followers misinterpret what their freedom actually means, and they take for granted what Christ Jesus did for us on the cross. Galatians 5:1 tells us, "Stand fast therefore in the liberty wherewith Christ hath made us free, and be not entangled again with the yoke of bondage." We must not take our position of being made free in Christ, and use this freedom as an excuse for sin. There is no excuse, nor is there freedom, in sin.

Some call doing whatever they please, "freedom." There is no freedom in sin, or doing, consuming, or saying anything that does not bring honor and glory to God. If it would not please God, *Do Not do it*, period. We have not been freed from the bondage of sin, only to continue doing what we have been set free from. I Peter 2:16 tells us, "As free, and not using your liberty for a cloke of maliciousness, but as the servants of God."

Freedom in Christ, is not an invitation to sin, because sin still creates a wedge between us and God. I Corinthians 6:12 (ESV) says, ""All things are lawful for me," but not all things are helpful. "All things are lawful for me," but I will not be dominated by anything." There is grace, but at what cost are we disobeying the desires of Almighty God? He is still holy, and still has a standard. We must still set the standard high, we must have Godly standards. There is freedom in obedience.

There is nothing that compares to the freedom that knowing Jesus brings.

~Patience

We live in a culture that promotes immediate gratification as superior to the beauty of waiting patiently for the fulfillment of anything. In our fast-paced culture, having to wait for anything is pretty much unacceptable. We have been conditioned to have an immediate gratification, fast food, mentality.

It is often hard to settle in, with a spirit of patience, and be still and wait. We tend to have little to no patience when driving, waiting on traffic lights, food preparation, decision making, relationships, people in general, and even God. But, If we are to shine the light of Christ in all we do, we must exercise patience.

Oftentimes, we miss what God has to teach us, or a blessing that He intends to extend to us, because we lack patience. We tend to take matters into our own hands, as opposed to waiting things out. If we would only allow the Holy Spirit to teach us patience, while waiting on the Lord, this attribute will carry through to the other areas in our lives. Psalm 27:14 says, "Wait on the LORD: be of good courage, and he shall strengthen thine heart: wait, I say, on the LORD."

If we would begin to seek the Lord, and pray for patience, as well as opportunities to exercise patience, perhaps we could more easily "be still and know that He is God." Psalm

46:10 tells us, "Be still, and know that I am God: I will be exalted among the heathen, I will be exalted in the earth." It would benefit us greatly if we would take time to cultivate our relationship with the Lord. Patience is required as we learn His will and His ways. We really have no excuse for our impatience, when we consider how incredibly patient God has been, and continues to be with us.

We should call to remembrance how patient God was, and is, towards us, when we grow impatient about anything, or with anyone. II Peter 3:9 tells us of God's great patience towards us, when it says, "The Lord is not slack concerning his promise, as some men count slackness; but is longsuffering to us-ward, not willing that any should perish, but that all should come to repentance." Christ is the perfect model of how we should exercise patience. Although He is persistently drawing hearts to Himself, He at the same time, is abounding in patience.

Jesus, through the power of His Holy Spirit, patiently pursues our wayward hearts. He loves us so much that even in our sin, He waits for us. We must only learn from His example when we are dealing with people, pursuits, and prayer. Patience is paramount in the life of Christ followers.

We, as Christ followers, must learn to wait. We have everything we require, from the Lord, to demonstrate self-control. God gives us everything we need, when we need it. Isaiah 40:31 "But they that wait upon the LORD shall renew their strength; they shall mount up with wings as eagles; they shall run, and not be weary; and they shall walk, and not faint." It is an exercise in humility to diligently wait upon the Lord, patiently. In doing so, we will in turn be able to do this with people, and situations in our lives. Romans 12:12 says, "Rejoicing in hope; patient in tribulation; continuing instant in prayer."

Patience is a virtue, and one of the fruits of the spirit. Additionally, the ability to wait without getting angry, frustrated, or impatient, is a demonstration of Godly character. James 5:7-8 says, "Be patient therefore, brethren, unto the coming of the Lord. Behold, the husbandman waiteth for the precious fruit of the earth, and hath long patience for it, until he receive the early and latter rain. Be ye also patient; stablish your hearts: for the coming of the Lord draweth nigh." God has placed His Holy Spirit within us; therefore, we are not lacking the power to remain patient.

The next time you are feeling impatient, unwilling to wait, antsy, or rushed, remember the great patience of Almighty God.

~The Infallible Word Of God

To know God is to know His Word. To effectively walk in His light, we must walk according to the path set out for us in the Word of God.

God's Word is unfailing, dependable, and always effective. God's Word is Truth. We can trust The Bible to instruct us in all righteousness and understanding. It is our manual for living, and all of our questions can be answered within the pages of the Bible. The Word of God draws us in, and solidifies our bond with our Lord and Savior, Jesus Christ. It does not change. It is His holy Word given to us. Nothing can thwart God's Word, because there is no limitation to its perfection.

The Bible has been the number one bestselling book in history, and it has been critically scrutinized and challenged over time. Ancient manuscripts of the Old and New Testament prove consistency and reliability. The New Testament also points back to the Old Testament. There are thousands of manuscripts with the message of Christ unblemished. Although the Word of God has been challenged, it remains undefiled and true. Isaiah 40:8 reads, "The grass withereth, the flower fadeth: but the word of our God shall stand forever." Matthew 24:35 says, "Heaven and earth shall pass away, but my words shall not pass away." God's Word endures forever.

The Bible was written over a span of some fifteen hundred years, by many authors. The authors who penned God's word at different times in history, maintain accuracy and consistency in their messages. The messages in the Bible are historically accurate, including the consistent accounts of Jesus throughout the Gospel books of Matthew, Mark, Luke, and John.

Every word written on the pages of the Bible were inspired by God. II Timothy 3:16-17 tells us, "All scripture is given by inspiration of God, and is profitable for doctrine, for reproof, for correction, for instruction in righteousness: That the man of God may be perfect, thoroughly furnished unto all good works." God's Word was inspired by Him. The entire Bible was God breathed. God used men to record His Word; therefore, they are not the words of men, but they are the Words of God.

We must believe, by faith, in order to receive what God has for us in His Word. To believe The Word of The Lord, you must know the Word of the Lord. The Bible is trustworthy and provides everything we need to live in alignment with God. Romans 10:17 says, "So then faith cometh by hearing, and hearing by the Word of God." In order to know, understand, and believe the Bible, we must read it, study it, and meditate on it daily. It is in this way that we truly grow in our faith and understanding of God's written word to us.

If we fail to study God's Word, we will not be able to follow His plan for our lives. II Timothy 2:15 shows us the importance of studying the Scriptures. "Study to shew thyself approved unto God, a workman that needeth not to be ashamed, rightly dividing the word of truth." Additionally, if we fail to study God's Word, we become vulnerable to the world, to the devil's schemes, and we will be easily deceived. The devil will trip us up, confuse us, lie to us, and accuse us. This is a guarantee. I Peter 5:8 warns us, "Be sober, be vigilant; because your adversary the devil, as a roaring lion, walketh about, seeking whom he may devour:"

Many believers find themselves confused, misled, bound to sin, and weak in their convictions, because they are Biblically illiterate. It is impossible to stand against the attacks of this world and the enemy of our souls, if we do not know what is written to and for us throughout the pages of the Bible. The main way that God speaks to us is through His Word. If we search Scripture, we will find answers to every issue, life question, moral dilemma, and so on.

We must read and study our Bible to know God better, and to know His purpose and plan for our lives. His Word guides us like a lamp to light our path. Psalm 119-105 says, "Thy word is a lamp unto my feet, and a light unto my path." We need to know The Word of God, so that it can guide and direct our steps. It is The Truth that instructs, guides, and helps us keep our eyes stayed on Christ. If we hide God's word in our hearts, our crooked places will be made straight, and we will be less likely to sin against God. Psalm 119:11 assures us, "Thy word have I hid in mine heart, that I might not sin against thee."

The Word of God is also part of our armor. We cannot stand against the schemes of the devil, if we do not know the Holy Scriptures. We have to do what Ephesians 6:17 tells us, "And take the helmet of salvation, and the sword of the Spirit, which is the word of God." Spending time in the Bible everyday will grow and mature our relationship with The Lord. Be sure not to neglect God's Word. It gives you power, strength, and resolve, to boldly approach each day, prepared.

It is impossible to know God, if you are not spending time with Him in His Word. The Word of God is powerful, life changing, and empowering. Hebrews 4:12 tells us, "For the word of God is quick, and powerful, and sharper than any two-edged sword, piercing even to the dividing asunder of soul and spirit, and of the joints and marrow, and is a discerner of the thoughts and intents of the heart." Get in, and stay in, The Word of God.

The Bible is our fully equipped tool box for living. Everything we need is found inside the Word of God.

~Fortify Your Mind

It is crucial that we are careful about what we allow to enter into our minds. Romans 12:2 tells us, "And be not conformed to this world: but be ye transformed by the renewing of your mind, that ye may prove what is that good, and acceptable, and perfect, will of God." What we habitually, casually, or even occasionally, grant access to our minds, will easily infiltrate our hearts. Isaiah 26:3 tells us, "You keep him in perfect peace whose mind is stayed on you, because he trusts in you."

To fortify a place (which in this case, is our minds), we must strengthen it with defensive works, in order to protect it against attack. II Timothy 1:7 says, "For God hath not given us the spirit of fear; but of power, and of love, and of a sound mind." We must guard our minds by saturating our minds with the presence of our Lord and Savior, Jesus Christ, as well as His truth. This must be our top priority, lest we fall.

We must be proactive, taking godly steps to secure our minds in Christ Jesus. Philippians 2:5 says, "Let this mind be in you, which was also in Christ Jesus." This does not occur naturally, because we all battle our sinful nature. We must, with the help of the Holy Spirit of God, purposefully protect our minds from ungodliness. This requires diligence and resolve. As Christ followers, we should be flooding our minds with The Word of God, prayer, and God honoring fellowship.

Just because certain behaviors, reading material, social media outlets, television programs, movies, and entertainment, are popular, or intriguing, does not mean they are beneficial or Christ honoring. I Corinthians 10:23 says, "All things are lawful for me, but all things are not expedient: all things are lawful for me, but all things edify not." We do need to discriminate and judge gingerly what and who we allow to influence our thoughts. Our minds must not be an open door to anything that isn't pleasing to the Lord.

This also includes who we are allowing to speak into our lives. II Corinthians 6:14 speaks truth to this, when it says, "Be ye not unequally yoked together with unbelievers: for what fellowship hath righteousness with unrighteousness? and what communion hath light with darkness?"

Obtaining advice and guidance on personal, spiritual, or financial matters, should not come from individuals, groups, or books, that do not honor Jesus, and biblical principles. Psalm 1:1 says, "Blessed is the man that walketh not in the counsel of the ungodly, nor standeth in the way of sinners, nor sitteth in the seat of the scornful." As harsh as it may sound, our sphere of personal influence, must not include unbelievers or ungodly propaganda.

We all must decide how much of ourselves we are willing to surrender to the Lord. When we fail to surrender all, including our minds, we fail to experience His fullness in our lives. Choose carefully who and what has any influence in your life, no matter how big or small it may seem.

Desire the mind of Christ.

~Compartmentalizing Your Faith

A compartment is defined in the Merriman Webster dictionary, as a separate division or section, or one of the parts into which an enclosed space is divided. To compartmentalize something is when we separate something, like our responsibilities, into isolated sections or categories. Sometimes people try to compartmentalize their lives. In doing so, they isolate the different aspects of their lives from each other, and none of the areas of their lives overlap.

For instance, a man might be a son, husband, father, midnight porn addict, business owner, Bible study leader, politician, and Christian. He may try to arrange things so that none of these areas of his life intersect. This will ultimately lead to breakdown and destruction. This is not God's plan for His children. We cannot mix evil with God's goodness. Even if he removed the pornography and still compartmentalized his faith, and isolated his relationship with God from the other aspects of his life, he would be displeasing the Lord. This never ends well.

In this example, if his Christianity flowed through and dominated all areas of his life, the porn addiction would not have had a chance to take root. Unfortunately, he did not purposefully keep Christ at the center of all areas of his life. As a result, he has a secret life of addiction. Even with the porn addiction removed, he would be opening himself up for attacks from the enemy of his soul, the devil.

We cannot be Christ followers and ban Christ from certain areas of our lives. In the event that we do, we are setting ourselves up for the power of sin to take hold, and we are most likely not intimately acquainted with the Lord. Psalm 86:11 tells us, "Teach me thy way, O LORD; I will walk in thy truth: unite my heart to fear thy name." As Christians, we should make certain that we are Not compartmentalizing our lives. We must walk in His truth, in all areas of our lives. It is a dangerous game of deception when we limit God in our lives.

Our beliefs, attitudes, behavior, and conversations, should always reflect our faith and trust in our Lord and Savior, Jesus Christ. We must not assimilate according to our environment, or who our audience is at the time. Matthew 5:16 tells us, "Let your light so shine before men, that they may see your good works, and glorify your Father which is in heaven." As Christ followers, we must always allow the Holy Spirit to manifest himself through us.

I John 2:6 says, "He that saith he abideth in him ought himself also so to walk, even as he walked." We must be consistently representing Jesus, in all areas of our lives. Christ wants all of us, not just parts, not just part time. Being a part-time Christian is not what God desires for us. He wants our whole heart, full obedience. He will bless those who faithfully follow after Him.

We must be consistent in who we are, and resist becoming someone else based on who we are associating with at the time. II Corinthians 10:5 says, "Casting down imaginations, and every high thing that exalteth itself against the knowledge of God, and bringing into captivity every thought to the obedience of Christ;" Our hearts and minds should be focused on the Lord, not on the world. The expectations of the world are not the same as the Lord's. James 1:8 says, "A double minded man is unstable in all his ways." In order to lead anyone to Christ, plant seeds of faith, or even have an effective witness, being open and authentic about our faith, is critical. To do otherwise is dishonoring to the one who saved our souls, Jesus.

If we have placed our faith and trust in Jesus, then our identity is found in Him. We cannot be a sometime Christian, or a matter-of-convenience Christian. The Holy Spirit should have dominion over every aspect of our lives. II Corinthians 5:20 tells us, "Now then we are ambassadors for Christ, as though God did beseech you by us: we pray you in Christ's stead, be ye reconciled to God." We are to represent Jesus well. Our love for Jesus, must be evident in every role that we have, and in every arena of our lives, both public and private.

Surrendering our all to Jesus, and fully submitting to His will and His ways, is a matter of obedience. If our desire is to please Him, we will welcome the Holy Spirit to reign and control every facet of our lives. Without the presence of the Holy Spirit of God in every compartment of our entire lives, we open ourselves up for the enemy to infiltrate our lives in those areas we withhold from God. The result is inevitably detrimental to our walk with the Lord.

We must allow God to be Lord of our lives, in every single compartment, and in every area of our lives. This is key to having a spiritually rich and fulfilling relationship with Almighty God. Grant God access to all of you.

~Not Ashamed

When we think about all that Jesus has done for us, how could we do anything else but testify? When we consider the eternal outcome for those who have not placed their faith and trust in Jesus, how could we remain silent? When we consider where we were before our surrender to the Lord, and where we are now, how could we shy away from sharing with others? When we ponder the immense love that He has lavished on us, we would be selfish not to declare the Gospel to all who will listen.

To be ashamed is to be reluctant to do something due to fear of embarrassment or humiliation. On the other hand, to be unashamed, is to act openly, without doubt or embarrassment. Let us be unashamed of the power of the Gospel, that saved our souls. Romans 1:16 says, "For I am not ashamed of the gospel of Christ: for it is the power of God unto salvation to everyone that believeth; to the Jew first, and also to the Greek."

To share our faith, God does not expect eloquence, or wordiness. He expects authenticity, humility, and truth. He simply desires to use us, to plant seeds of faith, mentor, and help usher others into the Kingdom of God.

There is no greater purpose, than to play a part in advancing the Gospel. In order for those trapped in darkness, to be set free in glory, they must hear Truth that leads to repentance. To hear, someone must speak. We must speak God's truth in love, to the hurting, lost, and imprisoned by their sin, guilt and shame. Let us be unashamed of the Gospel.

Yes, it is true, that the way we live our lives, is a testimony in itself. Matthew 5:15-16 says, "Neither do men light a candle, and put it under a bushel, but on a candlestick; and it giveth light unto all that are in the house. Let your light so shine before men, that they may see your good works, and glorify your Father which is in heaven."

Living our lives in a manner that reflects God's glory is only part of our commission from Jesus. In Mark 16:15, Jesus tells the eleven, "And he said unto them, Go ye into all the world, and preach the gospel to every creature." Christ died to pay the price for our sins, so that all who believe will be saved. We must not play it safe, and avoid ridicule, by only letting our lifestyle minister to people. How will the message of salvation be spread, if the children of God are not speaking the Word, in truth and love?

Good, well intentioned, unsaved people, often live moral, benevolent, and influential lives. This does not draw people to the saving knowledge of Jesus Christ. At the end of the day, these people are still unsaved, and far from God. We must share Christ with others, because He has changed our hearts and minds. We must testify, of the goodness of the Lord. Let's be unashamed.

We must not fear rejection, or alienation, as a result of sharing the Gospel of Christ. Jesus suffered more rejection, ridicule, and alienation, then we could ever fully understand, and He endured the cross, for us. Jesus is relying on us, His ambassadors, to share His message. The Holy Spirit will help us.

Sharing the love of God, is sharing the keys to life and freedom, which is only found in an authentic relationship with our Lord and Savior, Jesus Christ. Romans 10:13-14 says, "For whosoever shall call upon the name of the Lord shall be saved. How then shall they call on him in whom they have not believed? and how shall they believe in him of whom they have not heard? and how shall they hear without a preacher?" We are all called to be preachers, sharing the love of Jesus, unashamed.

Whenever God blesses us with the opportunity to talk about Jesus, and we are nervous or apprehensive, we must remember who lives in us. The Holy Spirit will give us the words to speak, will guide our thoughts, and be right there with us. Acts 1:8 says, "But ye shall receive power, after that the Holy Ghost is come upon you: and ye shall be witnesses unto me both in Jerusalem, and in all Judaea, and in Samaria, and unto the uttermost part of the earth." We must remember that Jesus is speaking through us. It is not us, but Christ manifesting Himself through us, to draw people to God. The Holy Spirit brings power, understanding, boldness, and confidence. Let's be unashamed.

It is important that we are open about our faith and trust in our Lord and Savior, Jesus Christ. We must always be prepared to share our testimony with others. There is no greater gift than the gift of salvation. I Peter 3:15 But sanctify the Lord God in your hearts: and be ready always to give an answer to every man that asketh you a reason of the hope that is in you with meekness and fear." The reason for our hope, is because of what the Lord has done for us personally.

Never be ashamed to tell of the goodness of God, and how everyone has been given the opportunity to spend eternity with God, in heaven. We mustn't withhold the way to secure the greatest gift ever given, the gift of salvation through the shed blood of Jesus Christ. Be eager to tell what Jesus has done for you.

~Unbelief

God always fulfills His plans and purposes. We tend to make hasty decisions because of our free will, but God can still use those decisions to work in favor of His divine plans. Our sinful nature wants to be in control. Despite the choices we make, whatever God's will is, it will be accomplished, it will come to pass.

Genesis 25:19-34 tells the story of the two brothers, Jacob and Esau. Abraham had a son named Isaac. Isaac married Rebekah. Isaac prayed to The Lord on behalf of his wife, Rebekah. She had no children, so God opened her womb, and she became pregnant. Genesis 25:22-23 tells us, "And the children struggled together within her; and she said, If it be so, why am I thus? And she went to enquire of the LORD. And the LORD said unto her, two nations are in thy womb, and two manner of people shall be separated from thy bowels; and the one people shall be stronger than the other people; and the elder shall serve the younger."

This was all part of God's perfect plan. Rebekah asked God for a revelation. She asked God why there was such turbulence going on inside of her. The prophecy would begin to be understood at their birth. Back then, there was probably no way of knowing that she carried twins.

When Rebekah gave birth, she had boys. The first to arrive, was red with a hairy body. They named him Esau. When the second baby came, he was grabbing Esau's heel. The name given to him was Jacob. As the twins grew up, Esau became a great hunter. On the other hand, Jacob stayed close to home, and tended to the sheep and cattle. Their father, Isaac, was partial toward Esau, and their mother, Rebekah, was partial toward Jacob.

As a result of impulsivity and a desire for instant gratification, Esau made a hasty decision. In Genesis 25:29-34 we are told, "And Jacob sod pottage: and Esau came from the field, and he was faint: And Esau said to Jacob, feed me, I pray thee, with that same red pottage; for I am faint: therefore was his name called Edom. And Jacob said, Sell me this day thy birthright. And Esau said, Behold, I am at the point to die: and what profit shall this birthright do to me? And Jacob said, swear to me this day; and he sware unto him: and he sold his birthright unto Jacob. Then Jacob gave Esau bread and pottage of lentils; and he did eat and drink, and rose up, and went his way: thus, Esau despised his birthright." Esau exchanged his birthright for a meal.

Many years pass, and in Genesis chapter 26 we see that much prosperity is gained for their father, Isaac. He was a very wealthy man. In Genesis chapter 27, Isaac calls for Esau, to ceremonially pass on his inheritance and blessing. Isaac, would like Esau to prepare him a meal, before he performs this very important ritual. Rebekah overhears this conversation between Isaac and Esau. Rebekah immediately devises a quick, but elaborate, plan to secure the blessing of the inheritance for Jacob instead of Esau.

She ignored the word from the Lord that was given to her, before the boys were even born. She helps Jacob disguise himself as Esau, going so far as to put animal hair on his neck and arms, because Esau was hairy. They successfully deceive Isaac, and steal the inheritance as well as the blessing.

Although, before their birth, God gave Rebekah a very specific prophetic word, her actions did not display faith in God's Word. Rebekah did not trust God. She had a spirit of unbelief, and therefore took matters into her own hands. Remember, Genesis 25:23 says, "And the LORD said unto her, two nations are in thy womb, and two manner of people shall be separated from thy bowels; and the one people shall be stronger than the other people; and the elder shall serve the younger."

God foretold what would happen. He specifically told Rebekah that she had two opposing nations within her, and the elder, Esau, would serve the younger, Jacob. Basically, this would have happened one way or another, for the outcome to be as God had said. Because of Rebekah's lack of faith, God had to use her bad choices to work together His plans and purposes. This is often the case with us as well.

It was only because Rebekah overheard Isaac and Esau discussing the birthright, that she urged Jacob to deceptively take it from his older brother. She wanted to make certain that she controlled the outcome for her beloved Jacob. How many times do we look past Almighty God, and try to take control? We, like Rebekah, are under the delusion that we can control things. We are not in control of anything, despite our stubborn efforts at trying. God is ultimately in control of all things.

How many times do we fail to wait on God to fulfill what He has already spoken? Or, how many times do we act, before seeking The Lord and wise Godly counsel. James 1:6 tells us, "But let him ask in faith, nothing wavering. For he that wavereth is like a wave of the sea driven with the wind and tossed."

We take matters into our own hands as a result of impatience, unbelief, and little faith. God is faithful. God will always do what He says He is going to do. We must trust Him, and wait on Him to accomplish what He says. We must choose to believe what God says. We must choose to wait on The Lord to fulfill His promises. We must let God be God, and trust Him. Proverbs 3:5-6 is a trustworthy promise: "Trust in the LORD with all thine heart; and lean not unto thine own understanding. In all thy ways acknowledge him, and he shall direct thy paths."

We must deny the spirit of unbelief at work in our lives. We must choose to believe the Lord, and rely on His faithfulness. We must remember that God is faithful and trustworthy. We can believe Him. Don't allow the enemy of our souls to seduce you with his lies. Believe God, and trust Him at all times.

~What Can We Learn From Jacob And Esau?

What price will you pay for a bowl of soup?

In Genesis 25:29-34 we are told, "And Jacob sod pottage: and Esau came from the field, and he was faint: And Esau said to Jacob, feed me, I pray thee, with that same red pottage; for I am faint: therefore was his name called Edom. And Jacob said, Sell me this day thy birthright. And Esau said, Behold, I am at the point to die: and what profit shall this birthright do to me? And Jacob said, swear to me this day; and he sware unto him: and he sold his birthright unto Jacob. Then Jacob gave Esau bread and pottage of lentils; and he did eat and drink, and rose up, and went his way: thus Esau despised his birthright."

Esau's birthright obviously did not mean that much to him. He failed to see the great future value and benefits of his birthright. He did not consider the significance, or weigh the consequences of this decision. Esau may or may not have been completely serious about exchanging his birthright for a meal, but his brother, Jacob, definitely was. You can be certain that Jacob knew the value of the birthright.

A birthright was reserved for the oldest son, and would go into effect after the death of the father. It included not only a very large double portion of the inheritance, honor, and family leadership role, but also a blessing over the birthright. For Esau, this would include the covenant that God made with Abraham, his grandfather, which would have been passed to Isaac and then to Esau. The Hebrew tradition was for the father to wait until he was nearing death to offer the blessing of the inheritance.

Technically, Esau acted deceptively as well. He sold his birthright to Jacob, and was planning to receive the blessing of the inheritance from their father, Isaac, anyway. Romans 12:2 says, "And be not conformed to this world: but be ye transformed by the renewing of your mind, that ye may prove what is that good, and acceptable, and perfect, will of God." He did not willingly tell his father about the exchange he had made years ago with his brother, Jacob. Remember, he was preparing to get his blessing of the inheritance, at the time Jacob was actually receiving it.

Esau made an impulsive decision, based on his temporary fleshly need, that would change everything for him. Our culture today, operates in a very similar self-absorbed way. The need for immediate gratification tends to trump sound judgement. Even Christ followers tend to act in this very manner, and live with the regrets and consequences, sometimes for a lifetime. Galatians 5:16 tells us, "This I say then, Walk in the Spirit, and ye shall not fulfil the lust of the flesh."

Seeking God's guidance first is not popular in our fast-paced culture. For Christ followers, our model for living and decision making should not be found by following the world's example. We should model Godly principles of self-control and patience. We must seek The Lord, before acting out in the heat of the moment. Jeremiah 29:13 is referring to Israel, but it is a Godly principle for all time. It says, "And ye shall seek me, and find me, when ye shall search for me with all your heart." Our flesh is weak and sinful, and cannot be trusted. Seek God, and He will direct you according to His will.

184

It is critical that we resist the temptation to act impulsively. The possible short- or long-term consequences are not worth the temporary pleasure. Many have destroyed future opportunities because of lack of self-control. The bowl of soup, is a bowl of deceit, and not worth it.

Galatians 6:7-8 says, "Be not deceived; God is not mocked: for whatsoever a man soweth, that shall he also reap. For he that soweth to his flesh shall of the flesh reap corruption; but he that soweth to the Spirit shall of the Spirit reap life everlasting." Yielding to a moment of weakness, focusing on immediate pleasure and satisfaction, or saying yes when we ought to say no, could potentially sacrifice or destroy our future. Proverbs 25:28 says, "He that hath no rule over his own spirit is like a city that is broken down, and without walls." We must recognize that nothing is worth sacrificing the future that God has planned and purposed for us.

I Chronicles 16:11 says, "Seek the LORD and his strength, seek his face continually." If we diligently seek after God, and keep our hearts and minds stayed on Him, He will keep our way pure before Him. Hebrews 11:6 shows us, "But without faith it is impossible to please him: for he that cometh to God must believe that he is, and that he is a rewarder of them that diligently seek him." He will make every crooked place straight.

When your flesh is trying to take control, remember that God is big enough, and worthy enough for you to resist. Momentary pleasure or worldly gain, is never worth the sacrifice or future consequences that follow. Don't allow anything to become your bowl of soup.

No soup is that good.

~How To Learn From God

God gives us the opportunity to learn from Him, by the impartation of truth, through His Holy Spirit. There are innumerable life lessons to be learned, if we will focus our attention on the Lord. He is worthy of our attention. Our God is an awesome God. He is our Father, and He desires for us to learn from Him. He has a way of teaching us through His Word, our experiences, and through our obedience.

God, through His Holy Spirit, teaches us from His Word. Joshua 1:8 tells us, "This book of the law shall not depart out of thy mouth; but thou shalt meditate therein day and night, that thou mayest observe to do according to all that is written therein: for then thou shalt make thy way prosperous, and then thou shalt have good success." Everything that we need to know about God, His will, His ways, how to be in right standing with the Lord, how to live our lives, and how to please Him, can be found in His written Word, the Holy Bible.

The Word of God, is our standard. II Timothy 3:16-17 says, "All scripture is given by inspiration of God, and is profitable for doctrine, for reproof, for correction, for instruction in righteousness: That the man of God may be perfect, thoroughly furnished unto all good works." The Word of God, is a believer's instruction booklet for living. It tells us exactly how to live our lives in a way that brings glory and honor to the Lord. It teaches us all about Jesus: His love, redemption, forgiveness, grace, mercy, and more. We must study the Word of God, believe what it says, and

186

allow God to transform our hearts and minds, as we hide scripture in our hearts. God's Word is our textbook, and God is our teacher.

God, through His Holy Spirit, teaches us through our experiences. God will use everything that we go through, and every experience, to teach us. Psalm 71:17 says, "O God, You have taught me from my youth, And I still declare Your wondrous deeds." Nothing that we have gone through, that we are currently going through, or that we will go through, is experienced in vain. God teaches us valuable lessons through our experiences. We learn how to trust Him.

If our hearts and minds are stayed on Jesus Christ, we will see Him magnified in some way, through each of our life experiences. Matthew 11:29 says, "Take my yoke upon you, and learn of me; for I am meek and lowly in heart: and ye shall find rest unto your souls." Our Lord and Savior, Jesus Christ, wants to play a role in everything we go through. He desires for us to learn from Him. Each experience that we encounter, good or bad, we must ask the Lord what He wants us to learn from it. If we are in alignment with His will, He will show us the lesson to be learned, in all of our experiences. Life is our classroom, and God is our instructor.

God, through His Holy Spirit, teaches us through our obedience. As we obediently respond to the Lord, He will establish us and keep us rooted in truth. Jeremiah 32:33 "They have turned their back to Me and not their face; though I taught them, teaching again and again, they would not listen and receive instruction." Through obedience, we must humble ourselves, and receive instruction from the Lord.

God calls us to be obedient. Proverbs 10:17 tells us, "He is in the way of life that keepeth instruction: but he that refuseth reproof erreth." We must be obedient to the Lord, and be teachable; as a result, we will learn. As we humble ourselves, and maintain a teachable spirit, we will learn valuable life lessons. In John 14:23, Jesus says, "Jesus answered and said unto him, If a man love me, he will keep my words: and my Father will love him, and we will come unto him, and make our abode with him." To keep Jesus' words, is to obey. We must obey His word, in order to learn and grow in our knowledge, trust, and faith in Him. Let's clothe ourselves in obedience, and learn from God.

God is our most valuable, dependable, and trustworthy teacher. When we submit to Him, and put on a teachable spirit, we can learn so much from Him. The Holy Spirit of God, will teach us all things through God's Word, our experiences, and through our obedience. In John 14:26, Jesus says, "But the Comforter, which is the Holy Ghost, whom the Father will send in my name, he shall teach you all things, and bring all things to your remembrance, whatsoever I have said unto you." God is always teaching; therefore, we ought to always be prepared to learn.

~Lean Into Jesus

There are times in our lives when we don't have the answers, or we are unsure about our purpose. It is easy to rely on Jesus when we are sheltered from tempting situations. It is easy to rely on Jesus when all is going as planned or expected. It is easy to rely on Jesus, when everything in our lives seem to be perfectly aligned with God's will for us. It is easy to rely on Jesus when there is no turbulence at all in our lives, and the lives of those we care about.

Trying times are guaranteed, and we should be spiritually ready. We must be prepared to rely on Jesus when we hit a bump in the road, or chaos strikes from out of nowhere. Our relationship with the Lord must remain grounded in Truth at all times, so when life throws us a curveball, we can remain standing, firmly rooted in Christ. He is still all that we need. We must lean into Jesus.

I say lean "into" Jesus, because we must be found fully immersed "in" Him. Don't get caught outside of God's will. Don't find yourself somewhere on the periphery. Secure yourself in Him, and be prepared to lean in even further, when trouble strikes. Lean into Jesus through all of the circumstances that come our way.

Lean into Jesus when temptation arises. It is a guarantee that the devil will use anything he can to cause us to fall out of alignment with the will of God. We must stay in the Word, stay prayed up, and diligently lean into Jesus. James 4:7 says, "Submit yourselves therefore to God. Resist the devil, and he will flee from you." If we have placed our faith and trust in Jesus, we have all we need to resist, flee, and say no, when faced with temptation of any kind.

I Corinthians 10:13 tells us, "There hath no temptation taken you but such as is common to man: but God is faithful, who will not suffer you to be tempted above that ye are able; but will with the temptation also make a way to escape, that ye may be able to bear it." It is our choice to either lean into what we are being tempted by, or lean into Jesus when we are faced with temptation. If our heart and mind are partially in the world, and partially focused on God, chances are, we will choose to sin. If we keep our hearts and minds continually stayed on Jesus, choosing righteousness will be obvious, and easy.

Lean into Jesus when doubt arises. Mark 11:23 says, "For verily I say unto you, That whosoever shall say unto this mountain, Be thou removed, and be thou cast into the sea; and shall not doubt in his heart, but shall believe that those things which he saith shall come to pass; he shall have whatsoever he saith." What is your mountain? God has not given us a spirit of doubt, but the devil thrives on producing reasons and circumstances to plant seeds of doubt in us.

When we sense doubt stirring up within us, we must immediately speak truth over the doubt. Proverbs 3:5-6 tells us, "Trust in the Lord with all thine heart; and lean not unto thine own understanding. In all thy ways acknowledge him, and he shall direct thy paths." We must be sure of what we believe, what the Bible says, and what our purpose is. Our hearts and minds must be securely fixed on Christ, our solid foundation. Doubt cannot take root in our lives. We must allow the Lord to root us in truth, faith, and belief.

Lean into Jesus, when your heart gets broken. Our hearts will get broken, whether it is over a severed relationship, betrayal, prodigal children, or something else. It will occur, and we must be ready to lean into Jesus. Psalm 147:3 assures us, "He healeth the broken in heart, and bindeth up their wounds." Circumstances in life can take their toll on us, if we are not continually leaning into Jesus.

We must allow Jesus to carry our burdens, comfort us, and heal our hurts. If we lean into Jesus when our heart is troubled, we can declare II Corinthians 4:8-9, which says, "We are troubled on every side, yet not distressed; we are perplexed, but not in despair; Persecuted, but not forsaken; cast down, but not destroyed." Jesus should always be whom we lean into.

We must walk closely with Jesus during all seasons of life, and rest in Him. If we remain connected to Jesus, who is our only source of truth, peace, hope, and joy, it will not be difficult to trust Him, in times of trouble. It is when we take our eyes off Jesus, that we begin to sink as a result of the cares of this world. It is when we take our eyes off Jesus, that we forget our purpose, which is to bring glory and honor to the Lord. Lean into Jesus, at all times.

~We Are Like Sheep

Sheep are very unique creatures. God created humans and sheep with similar behavioral characteristics. He likens us to sheep, because they exemplify the way we humans behave. I would not go so far as to say that sheep are stupid, but they do require quite a bit of guidance and direction. Sheep tend to follow each other, even when it means danger. Sheep are easy prey for predators, because they are naturally non-aggressive. Sheep are docile; therefore, they easily accept instruction. Sheep tend to wander away from the flock, and from the safety of the shepherd. Sheep are vulnerable, and need to be watched, tended to, and supervised.

Thankfully, sheep have excellent hearing, and they remember the shepherd's voice, and respond to it. We must use our excellent hearing, and respond to the voice of our Lord and Savior, Jesus Christ.

Isaiah 53: 6 tells us, "All we like sheep have gone astray; we have turned everyone to his own way." Isaiah was very specific in stating that we all have gone astray. Not only some of us, but all of us have stubbornly turned from God's will for our lives at some point, and believed that we knew better than God. We all have tried to take control, and navigate our lives on our own. Our flesh desires to be in control of our lives, and we want to try to go our own way. Our flesh gets in the way, and we decide that we know better than God.

Just like sheep, we have a tendency to go astray, and get lost. Psalm 119:176 says, "I have gone astray like a lost sheep; seek thy servant; for I do not forget thy commandments." When we stray from the Word of God, and turn from the truth that we know, we need to be drawn back by the shepherd of our soul. I Peter 2:25 says, "For ye were as sheep going astray; but are now returned unto the Shepherd and Bishop of your souls." We, like sheep, need redirection, and guidance.

We are like sheep; in that we are followers. It is easy for us to be overcome by the ways of the world, and the culture of the times. We do not like to admit that we are followers, but we are. If we are not careful, we can easily be misled and deceived. Acts 20:29 says, "For I know this, that after my departing shall grievous wolves enter in among you, not sparing the flock."

The enemy desires to lie to us, and destroy our lives. He wants to keep us far from God, and keep us in darkness. James 1:14-15 warns us, "But every man is tempted, when he is drawn away of his own lust, and enticed. Then when lust hath conceived, it bringeth forth sin: and sin, when it is finished, bringeth forth death." We must diligently seek wisdom and discernment from our Lord and Savior, Jesus Christ. We are less likely to follow ungodliness if we are listening to truth, and grounded in God's Word.

Without the Lord as our protection, we are vulnerable to the lies of this world, and the devil. We must stay in the Lord's pasture. Sheep are vulnerable, and so are we. We are all capable of being misled, deceived, manipulated, and exposed. We are susceptible to being led astray from the Truth of the Gospel.

As the Holy Spirit continually draws us to Himself, Christ followers need to draw near to God as well. Psalm 100:3 says, "Know ye that the Lord he is God: it is he that hath made us, and not we ourselves; we are his people, and the sheep of his pasture." We are vulnerable when we are forsaking worship, reading our Bibles, praying, and fellowshipping with other believers. If we have our feet on solid ground spiritually, we will be more likely to be invulnerable to the schemes of the devil.

We, like sheep, have good hearing, and good memories. When we go astray, and the Holy Spirit relentlessly pursues us, we must take heed, and listen. We must respond to His voice, so that we do not eventually tune out the voice of the Lord. We must return to Him. John 10:27 says, "My sheep hear my voice, and I know them, and they follow me:" There is no better place to be, than in alignment with the will of God for our lives. There is no better love than the love that Jesus has for us.

If Jesus is the Good Shepherd, then it is an honor and a privilege to be His sheep.

~Are You A Sheep Or A Goat?

In Matthew 25:31-34 Jesus, speaking in parables, says, "When the Son of man shall come in his glory, and all the holy angels with him, then shall he sit upon the throne of his glory: And before him shall be gathered all nations: and he shall separate them one from another, as a shepherd divideth his sheep from the goats: And he shall set the sheep on his right hand, but the goats on the left. Then shall the King say unto them on his right hand, Come, ye blessed of my Father, inherit the kingdom prepared for you from the foundation of the world:" He continues in Matthew 25:41 saying, " Then shall he say also unto them on the left hand, Depart from me, ye cursed, into everlasting fire, prepared for the devil and his angels:"

Are you a sheep, or a goat?

In parts of the world, because of breeding, we can now easily distinguish between sheep and goats. Before special breeding and hybrid animals became the practice, it was difficult to say if you were looking at a sheep or a goat. Throughout history, sheep and goats looked practically identical, but their shepherd could easily distinguish between them. A shepherd knows his sheep.

Upon close examination of their behaviors, and preferences, there are many things that distinguish them apart. Sheep are more social, and they like to stay with the flock. If they go astray, they get lost easily. Goats, on the other hand, are very independent. Goats enjoy doing their own thing, and they get into trouble. A shepherd will effortlessly separate the sheep from the goats. Jesus will separate the true believers from the unbelievers.

Matthew 25 is referring to the last judgement. Just as a shepherd can easily separate the sheep from the goats, Jesus will separate those who are truly His followers from those who are not. Many so-called Christians, are actually imposters. In Matthew 7: 21-23, Jesus says, "Not everyone that saith unto me, Lord, Lord, shall enter into the kingdom of heaven; but he that doeth the will of my Father which is in heaven. Many will say to me in that day, Lord, Lord, have we not prophesied in thy name? and in thy name have cast out devils? and in thy name done many wonderful works? And then will I profess unto them, I never knew you: depart from me, ye that work iniquity."

Going through the motions, being good, doing good, and mimicking Christianity, does not make someone a believer. Asking Jesus to be Lord of our lives, and placing our hope, trust, and faith in Him, makes us an authentic Christ follower. Jesus will separate the sheep from the goats at the last judgement.

At the final judgement, Jesus will come, and all of mankind will gather before Him. Jesus is the great shepherd, and authentic Christ followers are His flock, or His sheep. He will, at this appointed time, separate the true believers from the non-believers. On that day, everyone will stand before Christ, and everyone will be held accountable for their lives.

For those of us who have placed our faith and trust in Jesus, we will be placed on the right. Those on the right, will spend eternity in the presence of the Lord. Romans 10:9 says, "That if thou shalt confess with thy mouth the Lord Jesus, and shalt believe in thine heart that God hath raised him from the dead, thou shalt be saved." Those who might look like sheep, but are not, will be placed on the left.

II Thessalonians 1:8-9 says, "In flaming fire taking vengeance on them that know not God, and that obey not the gospel of our Lord Jesus Christ: Who shall be punished with everlasting destruction from the presence of the Lord, and from the glory of his power." Those of whom Jesus places on the left will face eternal separation from Almighty God. If you truly love Jesus, believe, and have asked Him to be Lord of your life, there is no need to worry if you are a sheep or a goat. If you are not sure, you can be sure.

Make certain that you are a sheep, and not a goat. Have you placed your faith and trust in the only One who has the power to save? Jesus, who is fully God, came to earth, as the sinless Son of God. He came to live, and then die, in order to pay the penalty for the sin of all mankind. He bridged the gap between us and God. Because of His sacrifice, we now have direct access to God.

In John 4:16, Jesus says, "Jesus saith unto him, I am the way, the truth, and the life: no man cometh unto the Father, but by me." If we believe that Christ is who He says He is, and we believe that Jesus died on the cross for our sins, and rose on the third day, and is seated with God in heaven, we can be saved. Ask Jesus to be Lord of your life, and you are assured that you will spend eternity with Him. Eternity starts now.

~When You Are Tempted

If we have truly placed our faith and trust in Jesus, and we are walking in the spirit, giving in to temptation is not an option. When we say that the temptation was too great, and we just could not resist, we are denying the power behind God's promises. When we say that our weaknesses are too overwhelming, and we buckle when presented with opportunities to sin in certain areas, we are saying that the strength of the Holy Spirit of God within us is not enough.

I Corinthians 10: 13 tells us, "There hath no temptation taken you but such as is common to man: but God is faithful, who will not suffer you to be tempted above that ye are able; but will with the temptation also make a way to escape, that ye may be able to bear it." We are without excuse when we cave under the pressure of temptation, because God is a way maker.

God will make a way for us to escape. When we are staring at the temptation, the situation for which we know better, we must choose Jesus. Because God knows us more than we know ourselves, He already has a plan of escape orchestrated, for when we meet temptation squarely in the face. We do not have to have a head on collision with temptation. We must choose to take the detour that God provides. God does not say, "if we are tempted," He says, "when we are tempted."

It is our responsibility, as Christ followers, to ready ourselves for battle. The battle for our purity, our focus, our time, our allegiance, our minds, and our hearts, is raging in the heavenlies. Galatians 5:16-17 says, "This I say then, Walk in the Spirit, and ye shall not fulfil the lust of the flesh. For the flesh lusteth against the Spirit, and the Spirit against the flesh: and these are contrary the one to the other: so that ye cannot do the things that ye would." We must be diligently walking in the spirit of God, and keep our hearts and minds stayed on Christ.

Our flesh is weak, but Almighty God is greater, is stronger than our flesh. Matthew 26:41 tells us, "Watch and pray, that ye enter not into temptation: the spirit indeed is willing, but the flesh is weak." We must diligently seek God through prayer, and keep watch. It is when we become lackadaisical in our walk with God, and in our perception of who He is, that we increase our vulnerability when temptation arises.

It is never a wise decision to drift away from prayer, Bible study, and fellowship with the body of Christ. Walking steadfast with the Lord takes effort and dedication on our part. Our freedom from the power of sin and death is worth keeping our hearts and minds focused on the will of God for our lives.

We must be ready, we must guard our hearts, and we must guard our minds. God is faithful, and He has given us everything we require to stand firm. He has filled us with His Spirit, and He has given us everything we need to remain victorious over temptation and sin. Remember, it is not God who tempts us, nor is it God who causes us to fall.

James 1: 12-15 says, "Blessed is the man that endureth temptation: for when he is tried, he shall receive the crown of life, which the Lord hath promised to them that love him. Let no man say when he is tempted, I am tempted of God: for God cannot be tempted with evil, neither tempteth he any man: But every man is tempted when he is drawn away of his own lust, and enticed. Then when lust hath conceived, it bringeth forth sin: and sin, when it is finished, bringeth forth death." Bottom line, do not get drawn away. Be aware, be in the Word, be in prayer, maintain accountability, walk in the spirit, and keep in fellowship with the Lord.

Finally, we must never be without our spiritual clothes. We must be clothed in the armor of God, at all times. Ephesians 6:11-12 tells us, "Put on the whole armour of God, that ye may be able to stand against the wiles of the devil. For we wrestle not against flesh and blood, but against principalities, against powers, against the rulers of the darkness of this world, against spiritual wickedness in high places."

We must be well equipped, and not give the enemy access to our lives. Decisions need to be made continuously, and we must continuously choose Jesus. Temptation will not have its way with us. We must be strong in the Lord, and deny our flesh, period.

When you come face to face with temptation, flee.

~Sin Is Oppressive

When it is over ninety degrees outside, and humid, being outside is horrible. Most people can hardly stand the heat. The stagnant hot atmosphere makes you feel weighed down. You feel weak, powerless, and you want to escape the heat. When we think there is nothing as oppressive as a humid ninety-five-degree day, think about sin. Think about the oppressive nature of being bound to sin. Sin is an oppressor.

We were created by God, in His image, with the sole purpose to bring glory and honor to Him. Isaiah 43:7 tells us, "Even every one that is called by my name: for I have created him for my glory, I have formed him; yea, I have made him." He created us with free will. Because the first man and woman sinned, we all have a sin nature woven into our DNA. This was not God's plan for us, but through our choosing, sin changed the landscape of our lives.

We were not created to sin, and because God's purpose for us is to bring glory to Him, sin in our lives is oppressive to us. Our hearts and minds were created to worship God, and cannot thrive in the oppressive atmosphere that sin creates. Even if we are spiritually blind, and fail to recognize the oppressive nature of sin, sin is still oppressive. Sin is anything that falls outside of the will of God. Sin is any and all things that we do that does not please the Lord. Sin is oppressive.

Without Holy Spirit discernment and power, Sin so easily gets us bound. We must be walking in the fullness of the Spirit to resist the lure of sin. James 1:14-15 warns us when it says, "But every man is tempted, when he is drawn away of his own lust, and enticed. Then when lust hath conceived, it bringeth forth sin: and sin, when it is finished, bringeth forth death." Sin is crafty, manipulative, deceptive, and becomes a master to many. Sin inflicts hardship, pain, and constrains the sinner. Sin is burdensome, it alienates, and it assumes great power and authority over us. Sin is an oppressor.

Sin wars against our spirit. Sin deadens our conscience, and overextends its welcome in our lives. Sin in our lives is similar to being ruled by a tyrant or a dictator. Sin causes death to the one it imposes itself upon. Romans 6:23 tells us, "For the wages of sin is death; but the gift of God is eternal life through Jesus Christ our Lord." If we are not walking in the light of the Lord, sin captivates us, we choose it, we become bound to it, we become slaves to it, and sin oppresses us. It is a horrible trap. Sin lies to us, imprisons us, chains us, blinds us, and wants to keep us from the truth. Sin is oppressive.

When we lose our focus, become self-absorbed, want more of the world, and become enamored by the things of the flesh, we turn a deaf ear to the Holy Spirit of God. Isaiah 53:6 tells us, "All we like sheep have gone astray; we have turned everyone to his own way; and the Lord hath laid on him the iniquity of us all." We choose to sin, but we can also choose not to sin. We can, through repentance, be set free from our oppressor. We choose to be held captive to sin.

We can choose freedom from the oppression of sin through the blood of Jesus Christ. Matthew 1:21 tells us, "And she shall bring forth a son, and thou shalt call his name Jesus: for he shall save his people from their sins." Being oppressed by sin, is a choice that we make. We are not forced to sin. We choose to sin. We must make a new choice, and come out from under the power of our oppressor.

Sin is oppressive.

~Freedom For The Oppressed

Being oppressed against our will is not the same as being oppressed by sin. For those who have been oppressed because of slavery, human trafficking, abuse, or a dictator, it is not due to the choice of the oppressed. Sin, on the other hand, holds us captive, because we have chosen it. Sin often begins subtly, increases in intensity, and becomes part of our lifestyle. When we come into agreement with sin, it pulls us away from the holiness of God. Do not be deceived, we are oppressed, even when we "occasionally," choose sin. Sin is oppressive.

Ecclesiastes 21:2 says, "Flee from sin as from the face of a serpent: for if thou comest too near it, it will bite thee: the teeth thereof are as the teeth of a lion, slaying the souls of men."

We must understand, God wants to rescue us, redeem us, and restore us. It grieves the Holy Spirit of God, to see us bound to sin, and drenched in shame. It grieves Him, because we choose sin over Jesus. We do not have to pledge allegiance to sin. The Holy Spirit of God supplies us with all that we need, to reject sin. II Corinthians 7:10 says, "For godly sorrow worketh repentance to salvation not to be repented of: but the sorrow of the world worketh death." We must choose spiritual life over death. We can respond to the Holy Spirit's conviction, turn from sin, and choose Jesus. Sin no longer has to have a hold on us. Choose not to be oppressed.

Sin oppresses us, as long as we allow it to oppress us. We must respond to the calling of Christ on our lives, and forsake sin. We must decide to live by the spirit of the Lord, and no longer obey the longings of our flesh. Our flesh is weak and powerless against sin, but God is all powerful and He has already conquered sin for us.

Galatians 5:16 tells us, "This I say then, walk in the Spirit, and ye shall not fulfil the lust of the flesh." This is another trustworthy promise. If we keep our hearts and minds stayed on Christ, remain steadfast in our study and application of The Word of God, and maintain faithfulness in prayer, we will not give way to our flesh. We will no longer choose sin, the oppressor.

We must make the choice to come out from under the heavy weight of sin, our oppressor. Sin no longer has to be our master. It is our choice whom, or what, we serve. We must not believe the lie of the enemy of our souls when he says we are stuck, we are too far gone, we are fine as we are, or when he tries to convince us that our sin is not even sin. Satan desires to keep us oppressed by sin.

God desires for us to say farewell to our oppressor, receive Christ's blood covering for our sin, and sin no more. I John 1:9 promises, "If we confess our sins, he is faithful and just to forgive us our sins, and to cleanse us from all unrighteousness." It really is that simple. Turn away from your oppressor.

Our Lord and Savior, Jesus Christ, is constantly pursuing us. He is in pursuit of all of mankind. He is patient, while He waits for us to answer the call He has placed on our lives. We choose sin; therefore, we choose to be oppressed. Sin binds us, shackles us, deceives us, tries to destroy us, and oppresses us.

Our flesh is weak, and desires to return to sin. The strength of the Spirit of God is far more powerful, and if we are willing, will keep us from sin. Forsake sexual sin, perversion, a lying tongue, gossip, greed, selfishness, drunkenness, and unwholesome talk.

Choose life in the Spirit. Sin does not have to be your master any longer. Choose Jesus, every moment of every day. Choose Jesus with every breath that you breathe. Say goodbye to sin, which is no longer your oppressor. Walking in freedom, apart from your oppressor, is a choice.

~Deny Your Flesh

We all have challenges that will be set before us, in our walk with the Lord. One of those challenges will be temptation. We must be prepared, clothed in the Armor of God (Ephesians 6:11-24), and willing to be held accountable for our lives. The challenge is to walk steadfast in the Lord, in all areas of our lives. We must be willing to be held accountable to God for our actions, whether in thought or deed.

We must stop blaming the devil for every sinful thought or deed that we commit in our lives. Yes, he does do his best to derail us, but we have power that comes from our relationship with Jesus, to keep our hearts and minds stayed on Christ. We are more than conquerors. Romans 8:37 tells us, "Nay, in all these things we are more than conquerors through him that loved us." Because of Christ, we are victorious. The battles of the flesh that we have faced, are facing, and will face, have already been won. We must lay claim to the victory we have over sin. Our Lord and Savior, Jesus Christ, has won the victory over sin and death. Walk in victory.

It is important that we remember to whom we belong, and the benefits we have received. We have Kingdom benefits, as a result of our faith and trust in Jesus. We have power over the devil, through the strength of our convictions, and our relationship with Jesus Christ. If we deny the power imparted to us to resist the devil, we then rely on our flesh. Romans 7:19 says, "For I know that in me (that is, in my flesh,) dwelleth no good thing: for to will is present with me; but how to perform that which is good I find not."

We cannot depend on our flesh to do the right thing. We cannot believe in our flesh, to keep our way pure. We cannot rely on our flesh to resist temptation. Our flesh is bent toward sin. Romans 7:25 tells us, "I thank God through Jesus Christ our Lord. So then with the mind I myself serve the law of God; but with the flesh the law of sin." Our flesh is unreliable. We need the Holy Spirit of God, intervening on our behalf. The Holy Spirit, who dwells in us, is reliable and trustworthy. The Holy Spirit, if we allow, will rescue us before we fall.

The devil takes advantage of every opportunity we afford him, to wreak havoc in our lives. We must actively stand against his schemes, and not render ourselves powerless, weak, or defeated, in his midst. Although quick at times, there is a process that sin takes. If we are aware, and always mindful of the presence of God in our lives, we can resist all temptation. We can always reject the opportunity to sin. We are without excuse, because we are not helpless victims of sin. No, we are mighty righteous warriors, who have the power of Holy God in us, to walk victorious over sin. Period.

We must take responsibility for our actions. James 1:14-15 says, "But every man is tempted, when he is drawn away of his own lust, and enticed. When lust hath conceived, it bringeth forth sin: and sin, when it is finished, bringeth forth death." There is a drawing away of our minds and our flesh, which leaves us vulnerable to sin. In that vulnerability, temptation arises. This is a challenge that will always be before us. We must choose not to be drawn away. We can be drawn away by a thought, a word from someone, something we see, or our own desires.

A choice has to be made. It is when we are drawn away, that we are tempted. When lust, or desire, has taken root, sin has been conceived. There is not going to be a temptation if we are not drawn away, and enticed. To be enticed is to be attracted to something, or interested to the point of action. Lust is a result of being enticed by the temptation. Lust is a selfish desire for an experience, thought, something, or someone, that ought not to be. The minute we are drawn away from godliness, we have sinned. Sin results in spiritual death.

If we are tempted, remember that Jesus will always offer a way of escape. We do not have to fall into agreement with any form of ungodliness. We do not have to be in agreement with our flesh. We must choose to turn our focus to Jesus when faced with temptation. I Corinthians 10:13 tells us, "There hath no temptation taken you but such as is common to man: but God is faithful, who will not suffer you to be tempted above that ye are able; but will with the temptation also make a way to escape, that ye may be able to bear it." God, through the awesome power of His Holy Spirit, always holds His hand out for us to grab. He will always make a way.

If we can grab hold of the reality that in our flesh resides no good thing, and cling to Jesus, we can walk steadfastly in righteousness. We will continuously be faced with opportunities to choose godliness. Keep denying your flesh, and walk in the spirit.

~The Devil is Real

We cannot properly stand up against our enemy, if we don't understand who our enemy is. We cannot flee from our enemy if we can't recognize him or his ways. We cannot break free from our enemy if we have come into agreement with him.

We tend to forget that we have an enemy in the heavenly realm that is very real, and wants nothing less than to see us hopeless, trapped in sin and shame, wrecked by our sin, torn to shreds by our trauma, and destroyed. We cannot ignore his presence, and we must stand guard. We must stay vigilant, with our hearts and minds stayed on Jesus. We must be aware of the ways Satan attempts to deceive us, so we keep ourselves from coming into agreement with the adversary of our souls.

God created us to be intimately connected to Him. Our own rebellion, and Satan's desire to keep us separated from God, has made this challenging. We must realize the power that the devil has. Although, greater is Christ who is in us, the devil wants to war with our flesh and soul. I John 4:4 tells us, "Ye are of God, little children, and have overcome them: because greater is he that is in you, than he that is in the world." We must remain actively connected to our source of strength, power, and truth. We must keep our focus on Jesus, and His Word. This is the only way to prevent the devil from slipping into our lives, and wreaking havoc.

We must understand who Satan is, and what his objectives are. Satan was an angel, and was unleashed in the world when he rebelled against God. He has been in opposition to God and man ever since. He knows that God desires us to be in right relationship with Him, through Jesus Christ. As a result, Satan uses everything he can to keep us from being and doing all that the Lord created us for.

Before we come to the saving knowledge of Jesus Christ, the eyes of our hearts and minds are blinded by our own sinfulness, and the enemy of our souls, Satan. It is the power of the gospel message of Jesus Christ, that causes us to respond to the Holy Spirit, who draws us to Christ.

Satan starts very early, using every means possible, to blind us to the Truth. II Corinthians 4:3-4 tells us, " But if our gospel be hid, it is hid to them that are lost: In whom the god of this world (Satan) hath blinded the minds of them which believe not, lest the light of the glorious gospel of Christ, who is the image of God, should shine unto them." Satan, the god of this world, works tirelessly to keep us blind to the transforming, saving power of the gospel of Jesus Christ.

It can be difficult to recognize Satan's tactics, or his hand in the circumstances of our lives, if we are not walking in the light of the Lord. Anything that opposes the Word of God, is not from God. We must keep our eyes fixed on Jesus, and exercise Godly discernment at all times, so we do not give way to the enemy.

Because we are all born with a sin nature, we are so easily inclined to fall into agreement with our adversary, the devil. Although the things of God are not hidden from us, our tendency is to go astray. Isaiah 53:6a tells us, "All we like sheep have gone astray; we have turned everyone to his own way." It is critical that we fall into alignment, and remain in alignment, with the Word of God, His will, and His ways.

It is through our unbelief, that the enemy has an open invitation to manipulate us, and snatch what truth has been sown, right out of our hearts, before it takes root. In the parable of the sower, and a few other parables found in Matthew chapter 13, Jesus tells his disciples how the enemy attempts to prevent the Word of God from being rooted in us, with every opportunity he gets. He is a deceiver, and will prevent us from hearing, immediately take away what we have heard, and even confound what we have heard with his lies, and with the cares of this world.

Often times, the enemy convinces us that there is no God, no devil, no sin, no moral absolutes, or even no real standard that we should live up to. Today's popular postmodern thought has us believing that each of us can create our own standards, do whatever we want, and live autonomously. Eventually, these attitudes and beliefs cause us to grow numb to the voice of the Holy Spirit; we reject biblical teaching, then we become increasingly bound to sin and far from the will of God.

We can deceive ourselves into believing that we do not need God, but, if our unbelief isn't turned into belief, we will never experience the abundant life. In John 10:10 Jesus says, "The thief cometh not, but for to steal, and to kill, and to destroy: I am come that they might have life, and that they might have it more abundantly." If we come into an agreement with the lies of this world, our flesh, and the devil, we will not live an abundant life in the presence of Our Lord and Savior, Jesus Christ. Do not believe the lie that we can live however we choose, and still be in right standing with God.

The devil speaks lies to us, and over us. This feeds life into the spirit of delusion and unbelief that keeps us far from God. The enemy of our souls is crafty, and uses people, ideas, culture, and more, to keep us in darkness. Unfortunately, we often don't recognize it for what it is. We either yield to Jesus, or we yield to the devil.

John 8:44 tells us, "Ye are of your father the devil, and the lusts of your father ye will do. He was a murderer from the beginning, and abode not in the truth, because there is no truth in him. When he speaketh a lie, he speaketh of his own: for he is a liar, and the father of it." Satan does not introduce himself, and ask permission to hinder us or keep us bound to our sin. His tactics are subtle and very deceptive.

When we are living our lives apart from God, we are not truly living. We are dead spiritually. The good news is when we enter into a relationship with God, through the shed blood of Jesus Christ, we are revived spiritually, and walk in newness of life. Satan was defeated at Calvary, and he only has power over us if we allow it.

Every moment that Satan is coming after us, The Holy Spirit of God is relentlessly pursuing us as well. Choose Jesus. We must reject all ungodliness, and cling to Jesus. To live an abundant life, we must come into full agreement with the Word of God, and His plan and purpose for us.

Romans 15:13: "Now the God of Hope fill you with all joy and peace in believing, that ye may abound in hope, through the power of the Holy Ghost."

At the name of Jesus, Satan must get out of our way.

~The Devil Is A Liar

We must familiarize ourselves with Satan's modus operandi (ways). Let's ready ourselves, with awareness and truth.

None of us, in ourselves; is strong enough, wise enough, disciplined enough, resilient enough, steadfast enough, brave enough, smart enough, logical enough, or reasonable enough to be victorious on our own against the wiles of the enemy of our souls, Satan. II Thessalonians 3:3 assures us, "But the Lord is faithful, who shall stablish you, and keep you from evil." How do we actively stand with the Lord, and not get derailed by the enemy of our souls? We must not only be firmly established in Christ, who has already won the victory, but also be entrenched in His Word.

Who is the devil, and why should we care?

God created everything. He created the heavens, the earth, animals, and He created man in His likeness. Everything that has been created, He created. Colossians 1:16 tells us, "For by him were all things created, that are in heaven, and that are in earth, visible and invisible, whether they be thrones, or dominions, or principalities, or powers: all things were created by him, and for him:"

Among God's created things, God created angelic beings to worship Him. One of those, an anointed cherub, did not want to submit to God, but wanted to be above God. He was "the seal of perfection." Ezekiel 28:15 tells us, "Thou wast perfect in thy ways from the day that thou wast created, till iniquity was found in thee." God created him as an angelic being, but he became Satan.

Because of Satan's rebellion, God cast him out of heaven, along with his angels, to make his dwelling and dominion on earth. Revelation 12:9 says, "And the great dragon was cast out, that old serpent, called the Devil, and Satan, which deceiveth the whole world: he was cast out into the earth, and his angels were cast out with him." From that point on, Satan's main objective has been to create doubt, deceive, and ultimately, separate us from the love and protection of God. Satan is cunning, deceptive, and he lies and accuses us. He is determined to "deceive the whole world," and keep us from the presence of the Lord. His plan is to keep us blinded to God's truth, and swallow us up in darkness. There is a real battle taking place. Satan has been deceiving man since Adam.

God created the first man and woman in His likeness. They had it all. Everything was perfect. God commanded Adam to refrain from eating the fruit of one tree. Why not eat from that one tree? Because eating from it would alert him to the knowledge of good and evil. God specifically said not to eat from it. In Genesis 2:16-17 God says, "And the Lord God commanded the man, saying, Of every tree of the garden thou mayest freely eat: But of the tree of the knowledge of good and evil, thou shalt not eat of it: for in the day that thou eatest thereof thou shalt surely die" The devil took this opportunity to create doubt in the mind of Eve.

Make no mistake, the devil is real, and he is a liar and a thief. He appeared to Eve, in the form of a serpent, and told Eve something like this, "go ahead and eat, you won't surely die. Don't you want to know the things that God knows?

Come on, eat." She ate. Oh, but then Adam ate! Bingo, sin enters the world through one man: Adam.

Although Satan rebelled and was cast out of heaven, and Eve tasted the fruit first, Adam was the one given the command. It was through Adam's choice that sin has tainted all of mankind. Romans 5:12 tells us, "Wherefore, as by one man sin entered into the world, and death by sin; and so death passed upon all men, for that all have sinned:" Adam and Eve disobeyed God, and suffered spiritual death, just as God had warned. They were lured into disobedience through the crafty deception of the Devil.

God created us with free will. Yes, the angels, Adam, Eve, as well as all humans are created with free will. Adam and Eve chose not to trust God. Instead, they were drawn in, and enticed by the prompting of Satan. They disobeyed God. In the same way, it is our choice to follow God, or follow our flesh and the ways of the world. The world that God created has been plagued by sin and rebellion since Adam's choice. We must diligently seek God, and His righteousness. James 4:7 tells us, "Submit yourselves therefore to God. Resist the devil, and he will flee from you."

We must choose whom we will serve: God or Satan. It sounds abrasive, but if you are not following the Lord, you are either directly or indirectly following Satan. We must resist him, in order for him to flee. Remember he is the Father of Lies, and The Prince of Darkness. John 10:10 reminds us of the choice we have, when Jesus says, "The thief (Satan) cometh not, but for to steal, and to kill, and to destroy: I (Jesus) am come that they might have life, and that they might have it more abundantly." We must choose.

God Has been relentlessly pursuing man, to reconcile us to Him from the time of Adam to the present. Unfortunately, the devil is also diligently pursuing us.

Everything in the Bible, from Genesis to Revelation points to Jesus Christ, the Son of God, as our Redeemer and Savior. The Word of God thoroughly discusses the crafty schemes of the Father of Lies, Satan. Do not be duped by the tactics of Satan, because he desires to keep us in opposition to God.

We must recognize with certainty that the Devil is real, and wants nothing less than to see us destroyed. We cannot ignore his existence, or we will be caught off guard when he strikes. The good news, is that we have all we need to walk in victory over our adversary, the Devil. We must cling to the Word of God. We must know and believe the Word of God.

We must speak Jesus' name over all situations and circumstances, and speak the Word of God in the face of all accusations and lies of the enemy. Additionally, I Thessalonians 5:17 tells us, "Pray without ceasing." Lastly, put on the full armor of God. Ephesians 6:11 tells us, "Put on the whole armour of God, that ye may be able to stand against the wiles of the devil."

We must not only be firmly established in Christ, who has already won the victory, but also be clothed in His Word.

Be diligent, be aware, and be encouraged.

~ Render Satan Powerless

Satan works diligently to keep us in darkness. On the other hand, Jesus, the lover of our souls, works diligently to turn our hearts to Him. He has done everything needed for our rescue and restoration.

Without Jesus, we are hopelessly lost. We seek ways that seem right, but nothing satisfies like Jesus. We earnestly search for purpose, meaning, and validation, but nothing seems to fill the void we all have in our hearts. All the while, Jesus is pointing us to Himself. He never gives up on us. He never stops pointing the lost in the right direction. He patiently waits to rescue us from the broad path that leads to our demise.

Matthew 7:13-14 says, "Enter by the narrow gate. For the gate is wide and the way is easy that leads to destruction, and those who enter by it are many. For the gate is narrow and the way is hard that leads to life, and those who find it are few" (ESV). It is through His love shown on the Cross, that provides the rescue. When our eyes are finally opened, we only have one thing to do, and that is to receive Jesus' gift of salvation. All that is needed for our rescue has been done, and Nothing else but our belief and acceptance is needed.

Jesus did everything for our salvation on the Cross. He, the sinless Son of God died to redeem us. He now sits at the right hand of God. He died to save us ; to rescue us. What was required for our rescue has already been accomplished.

In Luke Chapter 15, Jesus talks in parables about going after that one who is lost. In Luke 15:4-5, Jesus says, "What man of you, having an hundred sheep, if he lose one of them, doth not leave the ninety and nine in the wilderness, and go after that which is lost, until he find it? And when he hath found it, he layers it on his shoulders, rejoicing.

In verse 7 Jesus continues, "I say unto you, that likewise joy shall be in heaven over one sinner that repenteth." Then in verses 8-9 He talks about losing one piece of silver, and then upon finding the silver, in Luke 15:10 He says," Likewise, I say unto you, there is joy in the presence of the angels of God over one sinner that repenteth." To repent is to turn from our sin. So, let's repent, and no longer give way to the devil. He only has power over us, if we allow him power.

In Galatians 1:4, Paul speaks of Jesus, "Who gave himself for our sins, that he might deliver us from this present evil world, according to the will of God and our Father:" When we are lost in our rebellion, and deluded by the world and Satan, Jesus longs to deliver us. He is our deliverer. He chases after us.

God, through the Holy Spirit, begins relentlessly pursuing our hearts from the moment we enter this world. We do not actually seek after God until He has opened the eyes of our hearts and minds. Romans 3:11-12 tells us, "As it is written, There is none righteous, no, not one: There is none that understandeth, there is none that seeketh after God." We like to think we sought God first, but He does the seeking. Luke 19:10 tells us, "The Son of Man came to seek and to save the lost." He chooses us, and we, by an act of our free will, say "yes."

What happens is that at some point in His pursuit, the eyes of our hearts and minds are opened to receive what He has for us. This is the working of the Holy Spirit in our lives. We are enlightened by the truth of the gospel message. We then begin to seek what is missing from our lives.

That void we had in the past, is now filled with Jesus. We now have a desire for something more, something bigger than ourselves. We now long for God's planned, purpose filled, will for our lives. He opens our blinded eyes. We are no longer under the authority of the enemy of our souls. We belong to Christ.

We were not created to be apart from God. This is why we are so lost without Him. Our salvation, is a direct result of God pursuing us. Christ did it all. Our rescuer is waiting. The devil is a defeated foe.

~Get The Devil Off Your Back

The Bible tells us in James 4:7, "Submit yourselves therefore to God. Resist the devil, and he will flee from you" This is a powerful verse in scripture, that offers a praiseworthy promise, when we do two things. We must submit ourselves to God, and we must resist the devil. If we do those two things, In Jesus' name, the devil will flee from us. This is a promise, with two conditions.

It takes humility to submit to God. In order to truly humble ourselves before God, we must do two things. First, we have to lay down our pride, and secondly, we must gratefully receive and secure our position under God's authority. I Peter 5:6 says, "Humble yourselves therefore under the mighty hand of God, that he may exalt you in due time:" It is critical that we have a firmly rooted understanding of what it means to humble ourselves before Almighty God. We are unable to submit when we fail to clothe ourselves in humility.

When we recognize that we are nothing without God, that we are His creation, that we were created to glorify Him, and when we abandon our pride, it is then when we understand humility. It requires a spirit of humility, to submit our lives under God's authority. It takes a spirit of humility to allow God to reign and rule every aspect of our lives.

For the devil to flee, we must willfully submit every aspect of our lives to Almighty God. It is when we fully submit that we understand humility. II Thessalonians 3:3 says, "But the Lord is faithful, who shall stablish you, and keep you from evil." Submitting to God is bringing ourselves under the umbrella of His authority and protection.

When we submit to God, we walk in alignment with His Word, which speaks truth and righteousness over us. To submit to God, we must know His Word, and obey His Word. To know His Word is to understand who God is, and what it means to follow Jesus.

Knowing God's Word helps prevent us from being deceived by the lies of the enemy and the lies of the world. Whatever does not line up with the Word of God cannot be trusted. II John 1:6 tells us, "And this is love, that we walk after his commandments. This is the commandment, That, as ye have heard from the beginning, ye should walk in it." To submit to God is to walk in obedience to His will and His Word. This is how we keep the devil off our backs.

When we fail to submit to God, we are unable to resist the devil. We remain vulnerable, and leave ourselves wide open to attacks from the enemy of our souls. Submission to God, means we relinquish all control and authority of our entire lives to Almighty God. This includes our heart, mind, and behavior. When we submit everything to God, the enemy comes at us, but God fights our battles.

The second condition that must be met, for the devil to flee from us, is to actually resist the devil. We cannot ignore the devil, and think that he will leave us alone. He is persistent. It is critical that we are able to recognize when the devil is at work in our lives. He spends all of his time trying to derail us, tempt us, lure us, and lie to us. He is no friend of ours.

Under no circumstances should we ever entertain the enemy in any way. We must firmly stand in opposition to his attacks. In Jesus' name, we must use God's Word, which is Truth, to combat the devil's lies. We must resist every attempt the devil makes to get at us. There is absolutely nothing that the devil can offer us that we should need or want. Philippians 4:19 says, "But my God shall supply all your needs according to his riches in glory by Christ Jesus."

It is important to continually cultivate our relationship with the Lord. We must make sure that we are not walking in sin. Sin in our lives gives the devil easy access to our hearts and minds. If we have any unconfessed sin, we need to confess it. I John 1:9 tells us, "If we confess our sins, he is faithful and just to forgive us our sins, and to cleanse us from all unrighteousness." To seek after righteousness, is to resist the enemy of our souls.

We resist the devil, by walking in the Spirit. Galatians 5:16 says, "This I say then, Walk in the Spirit, and ye shall not fulfil the lust of the flesh." If we flood our hearts and minds with God's Word, and walk in alignment with Jesus, we will be able to recognize the devil's lies, and resist the enemy of our souls. There is no other option, other than to resist the devil, if we are walking closely with the Lord.

So then, if we Submit to God and resist the devil, he will flee. When we are walking in submission to God, and not giving way to the devil, we have authority over Satan, through the blood of Jesus Christ.

Satan's power is nothing compared to the power of Almighty God. I Corinthians 15:57 says, "But thanks be to God, which giveth us the victory through our Lord Jesus Christ." Do not give Satan an invitation to lie to you, steal from you, manipulate you, or destroy you. He is not welcome in our lives. Create an atmosphere of godliness, and truth, that surrounds you. Resist him at every turn, and he will flee. In obedience, submit to God, and resist the devil.

~In All Thy Ways Acknowledge Him

There are many Bible verses that are quoted over and over, to the point where they are almost viewed as cliché. These verses are well known, and recited by Christ followers, as well as those who have not placed their faith and trust in Jesus. Certain verses tend to bring universal comfort, encouragement, and hope to those who use them, as well as to those who hear them.

The book of Proverbs is a book of the Bible that was written primarily by King Solomon, but inspired by God. The intended goal for the reader of the book of Proverbs is stated in Proverbs 1: 2-4 when it says, "To know wisdom and instruction; to perceive the words of understanding; To receive the instruction of wisdom, justice, and judgment, and equity; To give subtilty to the simple, to the young man knowledge and discretion." The Proverbs give us daily wisdom and instruction for living our lives as God desires.

Proverbs 3:5-6 says, "Trust in the LORD with all thine heart; and lean not unto thine own understanding. In all thy ways acknowledge him, and he shall direct thy paths." These verses end with a promise, but begin with prerequisites to the promise being fulfilled. God desires to direct our paths, and He desires to bless our lives. In order for God to do these things, we have to submit to His will. We must rid ourselves of disbelief, and believe that God loves us, and has our best interests at heart. When we truly believe, it is easier to trust and surrender our all to the Lord.

In order for the Lord to direct our path, we must trust in Him with our whole heart. Jeremiah 17:7 says, "Blessed is the man that trusteth in the LORD, and whose hope the LORD is." As Christ followers, if we fail to place our trust in the Lord, we will have no peace, power, security, or hope. We can trust God, because His Word is completely true. He is trustworthy. He never changes. We do not have to worry about God changing with cultural trends or popular ideas of the times. Hebrews 13:8 tells us, "Jesus Christ the same yesterday, today, and forever."

We can trust the Lord because He is love. I John 4:16 says, "And we have known and believed the love that God hath to us. God is love; and he that dwelleth in love dwelleth in God, and God in him." In order to authentically trust the Lord, we must get to know Him through studying His Word, and prayer. We must be in fellowship with the Lord. It is impossible to truly trust someone who we do not know. In John 17:3, Jesus says, "And this is life eternal, that they might know thee the only true God, and Jesus Christ, whom thou hast sent." The more we know Him, the more we will depend on Him, and our trust deepens.

In order for the Lord to direct our path, we must "lean not on our own understanding." Not leaning on our own understanding means that we recognize our limited ability to understand the ways of God. We accept that His ways are higher than ours, and we must rely on The Lord to fill us with His understanding. God is always right, He is truth. He will never steer us wrong, nor will He ever lie. We can depend on our Lord and Savior, Jesus Christ. We must lean on Jesus for understanding, because our understanding is tainted by sin, our flesh, and the world.

Isaiah 55: 8-9 tells us, "For my thoughts are not your thoughts, neither are your ways my ways, saith the Lord. For as the heavens are higher than the earth, so are my ways higher than your ways, and my thoughts than your thoughts." Our understanding is limited, and we are unable to see the big picture of things. God has a panoramic view. We do not have the breadth of understanding and insight that God does. He is omniscient, and He knows all things. There is nothing beyond His understanding. When we trust in Him, His understanding will manifest in and through us.

In order for the Lord to direct our path, we must acknowledge Him in all our ways. I John 4: 15 says, "Whosoever shall confess that Jesus is the Son of God, God dwelleth in him, and he in God." We cannot partially obey the Lord. We cannot only invite Him into parts of our lives. He is an all or nothing God. We must relinquish autonomy in our lives, and give God all authority.

We must recognize, and approve of His Lordship in our lives. Acknowledging God in every aspect of our lives, both publicly and privately, is what the Lord desires of us in this verse. This is necessary in our walk with the Lord. Hebrews 10:23 says, "Let us hold fast the profession of our faith without wavering; for he is faithful that promised."

Let's commit to allowing Almighty God, through the power of His Holy Spirit to manifest Himself in every area of our lives. Allow Him to take hold of us, and direct our paths. His desire is that we will yield to the Spirit of God. God is God, and there is nothing too big or little for Him. If we read God's Word closely, for truth and understanding, we will notice that many of God's promises require our obedience. Let's make it our ambition to walk in obedience to Christ.

~ Our Thoughts

All of our actions and decisions, have their origins in a thought. Our thoughts are extremely powerful, and often dictates the trajectory of our lives. If we let a thought, that is a lie, or an accusation, marinate in our minds, it becomes a thought pattern. Thought patterns are recurring thoughts, and if these thoughts are negative, lies, or accusations, they are destructive. These thoughts must be discontinued. If we allow our negative thoughts to control us, we will be walking on unpredictable landmines throughout our lives. We must submit our thought lives to Christ.

It is imperative that we surrender our entire lives, which includes our thought-lives, over to our Lord and Savior, Jesus Christ. We cannot be trusted to filter our thoughts on our own. Our thoughts are where fear, anxiety, sinful acts of the flesh, worry, and every other form of disobedience begins. It all formulates in our thoughts first. Each time a thought crosses our mind, that does not align with the Word of God, or with what God says about us, combat that thought by speaking Truth over that false thought. Psalm 139:17 tells us, "How precious also are thy thoughts unto me, O God! how great is the sum of them!" We are not bigger than our thoughts, but God is. We must allow God to continuously recalibrate our thoughts to align with His.

We must literally take action against our negative thoughts. II Corinthians 10:5 says, "Casting down imaginations, and every high thing that exalteth itself against the knowledge of God, and bringing into captivity every thought to the obedience of Christ;" Casting down, and bringing, are calls to action. We are not told to bring some thoughts into captivity to the obedience of Christ. No, we must bring every thought into captivity to the obedience of Christ.

All of our thoughts are vulnerable to the lies of the enemy of our souls. Therefore, we must reject, we must forsake, every thought that does not speak truth. We cannot win the war in our thoughts by laying down and doing nothing. All of our thoughts must come into agreement with the Word of God. Let's take action.

The Holy Bible contains everything we need to win the battle over our thoughts. In order for our thoughts to maintain agreement with the Word of God, we must study the Word. We must pray the Word, when our thoughts oppose the Word and the will of God, when our thoughts try to deceive us, and when our thoughts lie to us.

We must come against every negative thought, with Truth. Instantly, pray the thought into submission to God. If we know the Word, we will be able to identify misaligned thoughts. Hebrews 4:12 tells us, "For the word of God is quick, and powerful, and sharper than any two-edged sword, piercing even to the dividing asunder of soul and spirit, and of the joints and marrow, and is a discerner of the thoughts and intents of the heart." The Holy Spirit will guide us into all Truth, through God's Word.

Each time a negative thought creeps into our minds, speak to it. Tell that thought that he is an unwelcome intruder, and In the name of Jesus; he must leave. Begin to pray, worship, and speak the Truth, found in Scripture, over your thoughts, out loud. Speak the Truth of God's Word, and it will set your thoughts free. Isaiah 26:3 says, "Thou wilt keep him in perfect peace, whose mind is stayed on thee: because he trusteth in thee." Let's slay those disruptive thoughts. Luke 1:27 affirms, "For with God nothing shall be impossible."

Through the wondrous workings of the Holy Spirit, and the Word of God, we can subdue, overthrow, and maintain power and authority over our thought life.

Our thoughts must align with His thoughts.

~Take Every Thought Captive

In II Corinthians 10:5, Paul says, "Casting down imaginations, and every high thing that exalteth itself against the knowledge of God, and bringing into captivity every thought to the obedience of Christ." Before we talk about this specific verse, it is important to get a better understanding of what is warring in our minds. In order for our thoughts to align with the thoughts of Jesus, we must take every thought captive.

We must back up a few verses in II Corinthians 10, and get a proper understanding of what precedes verse 5. Paul is educating on the reality of spiritual warfare, and the manner with which we engage in battle. It is important that we know how to win this war. We must ready ourselves, to take every thought captive.

In II Corinthians 10:3, Paul writes, "For though we walk in the flesh, we do not war after the flesh." He wants us to understand that God is perfectly aware of our affliction. We are born with a sin nature, and although we follow after Jesus, we still carry our flesh around. In our flesh there is no good thing; therefore, no good thing can come from it.

Because of our flesh, we still have to deal with our weaknesses, our misgivings, our limitations, and our basic humanness. In and of ourselves, without the Holy Spirit acting on our behalf, we are not capable of slaying the sin in our lives, the thoughts that lead to sin and shame, the lies of the enemy, or anything that comes against us. Romans 7:23 says, "But I see another law in my members, warring against the law of my mind, and bringing me into captivity to the law of sin which is in my members." We cannot, on our own, win the war over our mind.

Because of the blood of Jesus, and the Holy Spirit who dwells within us, we do not engage the enemy of our souls, and of our minds, the way the world does. We enlist the Lord, Jesus Christ, by the power of His Holy Spirit, to engage in battle on our behalf. We must release the hold we have on our thought lives, over to Jesus. He has already won the victory; therefore, we ought to call upon Him, knowing that He will subdue the enemy of our minds.

Verse 4 tells us, "For the weapons of our warfare are not carnal, but mighty through God to the pulling down of strong holds." Our weapons are not worldly. Our weapons are prayer, Bible study, obedience to God, yielding to the Holy Spirit, Truth, and faith. These demolish strongholds of sin, shame, addiction, fear, our thoughts that try to wear us down, etc. We must not be ignorant concerning the power of the Holy Spirit to cast down strongholds, and every evil thing that comes against us, in the name of Jesus.

Now, in order for the Holy Spirit of God to be free to do what the Holy Spirit of God does, we must take every though captive. We must be obedient, and believe that we are incapable of slaying the giants in our lives, and of our thoughts, without the Holy Spirit. II Corinthians 10:5 says, "Casting down imaginations, and every high thing that exalteth itself against the knowledge of God, and bringing into captivity every thought to the obedience of Christ." Any thought that opposes the Word of God, must be dissolved.

This is done by combating lies with Truth. We must not give way to the devil, in thought or deed. Our thoughts must align with the will of God for our lives.

Every thought must be filtered through the Word of God. If our thoughts do not align with the Word of God, they must be obliterated. Not only must our actions and words be in obedience to Christ, but also our thoughts. Philippians 4:8 says, "Finally, brethren, whatsoever things are true, whatsoever things are honest, whatsoever things are just, whatsoever things are pure, whatsoever things are lovely, whatsoever things are of good report; if there be any virtue, and if there be any praise, think on these things." Our thought-life affects every aspect of our lives. Through them can flow poison, or rivers of life. Let rivers of life, and truth, flow from our thoughts.

Our thoughts belong to the Lord.

~Secure The Perimeter

Let's be strong in the Lord, and fortify our perimeter.

As Christ followers, there must be a higher standard for our lives. A call to righteousness has been placed over us. God has called us out of the darkness, and into the light. We must be prepared in and out of season to stand firmly rooted in the faith, lest we fall prey to the schemes of the enemy: even our flesh.

God's calling on our lives is to be set apart, sanctified, and made new. I Peter 1: 15-16 tells us, "But as he which hath called you is holy, so be ye holy in all manner of conversation; Because it is written, Be ye holy; for I am holy." God has given us everything needed to guard against sinning, at the moment we were saved; His Holy Spirit dwelling in us. It is imperative that we allow the Holy Spirit to manifest Himself in and through us. It is our responsibility to guard the perimeter of the closed figure, and that boundary is our refuge, our haven. We belong to God, and have so much worth fighting for. Before placing our trust in Jesus, there was a war waging in the heavenly places to keep us far from God, and bound to the power of sin in our lives. The moment we accepted Christ into our hearts, and onto the throne of our lives, another battle began.

This new battle is Satan's attempt to draw you back into the life you forsook to follow Christ. I Peter 5:8 warns, "Be sober, be vigilant; because your adversary the devil, as a roaring lion, walketh about, seeking whom he may devour." We must actively guard and protect the perimeter of our lives, our hearts, and our minds, in order to ward off the underhanded, and at times blatant taunting of the enemy of our souls. This includes the ungodly desires of our flesh.

Matthew 2:41 admonishes, "Watch and pray, that ye enter not into temptation: the spirit indeed is willing, but the flesh is weak." Keeping sin far from us takes effort on our part. We do not want any breaches in our perimeter. In order to prevent any fractures or rifts in our perimeter, there are a few things we must continuously, and consciously do. With the help of the Holy Spirit, we will secure our perimeter, and walk in pure freedom.

We secure our perimeter by believing in and trusting Jesus. As a result, we must spend quality time cultivating our relationship with Christ every day. We must meditate on the Word of God day and night. Psalm 1:2 says, "But his delight is in the Law of the Lord; and in his law doth he meditate day and night." Joshua gave similar instructions in Joshua 1:8. Saturating our hearts and minds in Truth is the best first step to keeping our perimeter sound. We must be fully devoted to the call that God has on our lives. By continuously doing these things, we will develop an undivided devotion to God.

We secure our perimeter by putting to death the deeds of the body. Romans 8:12-13 tells us," Therefore, brethren, we are debtors, not to the flesh, to live after the flesh. For if ye live after the flesh, ye shall die: but if ye through the Spirit do mortify the deeds of the body, ye shall live." When we deliberately forsake our flesh, we do not entertain sin. We must quickly identify any sin in our lives, even in our thought life. Sin is deceptive, and the Devil is a thief and a liar. The cliché, "Easier said than done," is a lie from the pit of hell. If we truly desire righteousness void of the presence of sin in our lives, fortify the perimeter. Do not allow sin to enter in. We must commit to giving the devil, sin, and our flesh no eminence.

Finally, we secure our perimeter by proclaiming the preeminence of God, and exalting Christ in all we do. Extend your thoughts and praise to Him at all times. Psalm 34:3 says, "O magnify the Lord with me, and let us exalt His name together. Being in constant communion with the Lord, leaves no room for Satan. Exalt the Lord, and let's keep our hearts and minds stayed on Him. Isaiah 25:1 sums it up beautifully, "O Lord, thou art my God; I will exalt thee, I will praise thy name; for thou hast done wonderful things; thy counsels of old are faithfulness and truth."

Be steadfast in your faith, and do not compromise your perimeter.

~Firmly Established In Truth

In order to find ourselves firmly rooted in God's Word, and fully relying on His Truth, we must consistently study the Bible, and hide God's Word in our hearts. Psalm 1:2-3 says, "But his delight is in the law of the Lord; and in his law doth he meditate day and night. And he shall be like a tree planted by the rivers of water, that bringeth forth his fruit in his season; his leaf also shall not wither; and whatsoever he doeth shall prosper." God's Word is nourishment for the heart, mind, and soul. It keeps us, and it sustains us.

How well acquainted are you with God's story? Do you understand, and believe, what is found within the pages of Scripture? Do you really know how to use the Word of God as a sword in this very real battle? Do you comprehend how powerful God's Word truly is? Do you say that you love God, but spend little, or no time, in His Word?

In order to know Jesus, and the power of His resurrection (Philippians 3:10), we must study the meat of His Word. We must continually grow in our knowledge, understanding, and pursuit of God's Word. In order to stand equipped, and grounded in our convictions, we must know what we believe and why we believe it. We must be firmly rooted in the Word of God.

Ephesians 6:12 tells us, "For we wrestle not against flesh and blood, but against principalities, against powers, against the rulers of the darkness of this world, against spiritual wickedness in high places." There is a battle taking place in the heavenly places for our heart, mind, and soul. Forces of evil are lurking, vying for our affection, attention, and our devotion. In readiness to respond, it is critical that we "Keep thy heart with all diligence; for out of it are the issues of life" (Proverbs 4:23).

Additionally, being immersed in the Word of God, positions us to obtain an error-free and objective view of God, the human condition, our role as Christ followers, the world view, and the battle that wages for our souls. When we are unfamiliar with God's principles and expectations laid out in scripture, we are not equipped to be a light in this dark world, and we are vulnerable to become easily confounded. We must be firmly rooted in the Word of God.

Romans 12:1-2 urges, "I beseech you therefore, brethren, by the mercies of God, that ye present your bodies a living sacrifice, holy, acceptable unto God, which is your reasonable service. And be not conformed to this world: but be ye transformed by the renewing of your mind, that ye may prove what is that good, and acceptable, and perfect, will of God." We renew our minds by meditating on God's Word. The Holy Spirit of God meets us at the table, when we study our Bible.

The Holy Spirit illuminates God's intentions toward us, nourishes our soul, and gives us wisdom, each time we draw near to God through the study of His Word. It is the Holy Spirit of God, our divine helper, who opens the eyes of our understanding. The Holy Spirit helps us, as we learn from God's Word, to bring our attitudes, behavior, and beliefs into alignment with God's will. When we apply God's Word to our lives, we will be better able to present your bodies a living sacrifice, holy, acceptable unto God.

If you truly know the Lord, you will read, be able to understand God's Word, and apply it to your life. I Corinthians 2:13-14 tells us, "Which things also we speak, not in the words which man's wisdom teacheth, but which the Holy Ghost teacheth; comparing spiritual things with spiritual. But the natural man receiveth not the things of the Spirit of God: for they are foolishness unto him: neither can he know them, because they are spiritually discerned." We are only capable of being established in Truth, when we know Jesus.

In order to possess godly wisdom and discernment, we must know the Lord personally, and we must know His Word, which is absolute Truth. II Timothy 3:16-17 says, "All scripture is given by inspiration of God, and is profitable for doctrine, for reproof, for correction, for instruction in righteousness: That the man of God may be perfect, thoroughly furnished unto all good works."

In Ephesians 4: 14 Paul admonishes the church about the importance of knowing the Word, and being mature, equipped with sound Biblical truth, "That we henceforth be no more children, tossed to and fro, and carried about with every wind of doctrine, by the sleight of men, and cunning craftiness, whereby they lie in wait to deceive." If your Biblical understanding is shallow, you are in a very vulnerable place. You are left open to being easily misled by false teaching or half-truths. Don't merely read, but study the Word of God. In doing so, your faith will strengthen, your confidence in what you believe will increase, your understanding of Christ will soar, and you will desire more of Christ in your life.

We will stand firm, we will not waiver, and we will be effective; when we are firmly rooted in God's Word.

~Eyes Wide Open

Only the Holy Spirit of God can open the eyes of the spiritually blind.

We are all blind to the truth of the Gospel, until by faith, we respond to the drawing of the Holy Spirit of God. There must be a point in our lives when we surrender to God. There must be a moment when we turn from sin, and submit our lives to Jesus. Until we do this, we are spiritually blind. Until we do this, we lack understanding of the things of God. Even those who claim that they have always been a Christian have to come to a point of total surrender. We are all spiritually blind until the moment the Holy Spirit of God opens the eyes of our hearts and minds, to the truth of The Gospel of Jesus Christ.

As I think back to when I was spiritually blind, I can definitely say that the enemy of our souls was working diligently to keep me blinded to the love of God. Even though I could see, I could not truly see. Even though I heard the Gospel message many times, I did not hear. Matthew 13:13 says, "Therefore speak I to them in parables: because they seeing see not; and hearing they hear not, neither do they understand."

My blindness was initiated by my sin, activated by disappointment, followed by pride, leading to a sinful lifestyle. The devil had a hold of me, and I was consumed with the lies of the enemy, telling me that I was worthless, too far gone, and not good enough. These were lies, not only in regards to my life, but about the character of God.

As we look at Mark chapter 10, we read about blind Bartimaeus. He was a blind beggar who God had been drawing to Himself. As Bartimaeus responded to the drawing of Christ, he acted in faith, as he cried out to Jesus to restore his sight. Mark 10:47 says, "And when he heard that it was Jesus of Nazareth, he began to cry out, and say, Jesus, thou son of David, have mercy on me." Jesus called him to Himself. Mark 10:51 says, "And Jesus answered and said unto him, What wilt thou that I should do unto thee? The blind man said unto him, Lord, that I might receive my sight." Because of Bartimaeus' faith, Jesus restored his sight, instantly.

Because of our sin nature, we choose darkness instead of light. John 3:19 tells us, "And this is the condemnation, that light is come into the world, and men loved darkness rather than light, because their deeds were evil." The devil desires nothing less than to keep us from the light of the Lord. We satisfy him when we choose to follow darkness. II Corinthians 4:4 says, "In whom the god of this world hath blinded the minds of them which believe not, lest the light of the glorious gospel of Christ, who is the image of God, should shine unto them." Furthermore, I Corinthians 2:14 tells us, "But the natural man receiveth not the things of the Spirit of God: for they are foolishness unto him: neither can he know them, because they are spiritually discerned."

We are all spiritually blind. We are blind spiritually until we responded to the drawing of the Holy Spirit of God upon our hearts.

None of us are too far gone, worthless, or inadequate. The enemy uses anything and anyone, to keep us blind, and in the dark. 2II Corinthians 4:3-4 says, "But if our gospel be hid, it is hid to them that are lost: In whom the god of this world hath blinded the minds of them which believe not, lest the light of the glorious gospel of Christ, who is the image of God, should shine unto them." The devil is a liar, and we must know and believe the truth. God is forever pursuing us. God is forever drawing us to Him. God opens the eyes of the blind.

The devil desires nothing less than to keep us from the light of the Lord, and he works tirelessly to do so. II Corinthians 4:4 says, "In whom the god of this world hath blinded the minds of them which believe not, lest the light of the glorious gospel of Christ, who is the image of God, should shine unto them." Furthermore, I Corinthians 2:14 tells us, "But the natural man receiveth not the things of the Spirit of God: for they are foolishness unto him: neither can he know them, because they are spiritually discerned." Jesus is bigger than the plans of the devil.

The devil does not only deceive, entice, and blind nonbelievers, but also believers. We must know God's Word, and walk closely with the Lord, so we do not get blinded by the schemes of Satan. Keeping the eyes of our hearts and minds steadfast on Jesus and His Word, is our security. Those who are blind, and who are unable to understand the things of God, can repent of their unbelief, ask Jesus to be Lord of their lives, and receive sight.

We must, by an act of our will, and by faith, choose Christ. When the Holy Spirit of God illuminates our sinfulness, we must act quickly. We must ask the Lord's forgiveness, and surrender our will for His. When we respond in obedience, a miracle takes place. Jesus opens our blind eyes. We are now able to see the love of God. We recognize our need for Him to be Lord of our lives, and we are born again spiritually. Ephesians 1:18 tells us, "The eyes of your understanding being enlightened; that ye may know what is the hope of his calling, and what the riches of the glory of his inheritance in the saints," He opens the eyes of our hearts and minds when we are ready to receive life everlasting.

Jesus came to save us from the penalty of our sin, and also to place judgement on sin. His Holy Spirit pursues us, but we must respond with surrendered hearts. He will give us over to our wicked ways if we continually deny Him. Speaking of those who actually witnessed Jesus' miracles, and still did not believe, John 12:40 says, "He hath blinded their eyes, and hardened their heart; that they should not see with their eyes, nor understand with their heart, and be converted, and I should heal them."

As for those who turn from their sin, and trust in Jesus, He will open the eyes of their hearts and minds, and they will be saved. Their eyes will be opened to the Truth, and they will see God rightly. In John 9:39 Jesus says, "And Jesus said, For judgment I am come into this world, that they which see not might see; and that they which see might be made blind." For those who think they have the truth according to their own version of truth, they will remain blinded. We remain blind when we refuse to trade our false truth for the Truth of the Gospel of Jesus Christ. We do not have to remain spiritually blind. We must choose to have our spiritual eyes open. We must choose Jesus.

Psalm 146:8 tells us, "The Lord openeth the eyes of the blind: The Lord raiseth them that are bowed down: the Lord loveth the righteous."

~ Ambiguous Gray

Many well-meaning Christians, as well as theologians, consider certain areas of thought and behavior not directly addressed in God's Word to be "gray" areas. Consider with me, the idea that "gray" is dark. Gray is defined as dull, lacking brightness, and vaguely defined. Nowhere in the Bible are we told to walk in the "gray." We are clearly called out of darkness, and into the light. Ephesians 5:11 says, "And have no fellowship with the unfruitful works of darkness, but rather reprove them."

I am convinced that these "gray" or ambiguous, unfruitful areas that we hear about, are areas that the enemy attempts to keep Christians walking in. I Corinthians 14:13 assures us that God is not the author of confusion. These "gray" areas we speak of are confounding, and a place we find ourselves when our flesh desires to dabble in the secular. Justifying our behavior by saying we have freedom in these gray areas is simply an excuse to keep our toes in the world. There is no freedom walking in the gray; freedom only comes when we walk in the light of the Lord. John 8:12 says, "Then spake Jesus again unto them, saying, I am the light of the world: he that followeth me shall not walk in darkness, but shall have the light of life."

II Corinthians 5:17 says, "Therefore if any man be in Christ, he is a new creature: old things are passed away; behold, all things are become new." We should desire godliness. When we are saved, our desire to blend in with the world should cease. What do light and darkness have in common? I Peter 2:9 reads, "But ye are a chosen generation, a royal priesthood, an holy nation, a peculiar people; that ye should shew forth the praises of him who hath called you out of darkness into his marvelous light."

We are called to be set apart. If our behavior is so similar to that of the world that a distinction can barely be found, we are not set apart. II Corinthians 6:17 tells us, "Wherefore come out from among them, and be ye separate, saith the Lord, and touch not the unclean thing; and I will receive you."

Our flesh wants to make provision for our flesh. Romans 13:14 says, "But put ye on the Lord Jesus Christ, and make not provision for the flesh, to fulfil the lusts thereof." When we place behaviors in the "gray areas," that are moral issues, our flesh is at work. Choices that have no spiritual implications are preferences. For example, what car to buy, where to live, what job to accept, or where to attend college, are decisions that are not moral or spiritual in nature. These choices are not what we are discussing.

Any behavioral decision that has any moral implications, are not "gray," and require a spiritual compass. Examples would be the following: Should I drink alcohol? Should I smoke? Should I go to a dance club? Should I ... fill in the blank. These are the types of behaviors we are discussing.

I Corinthians 10:23 says, "All things are lawful for me, but all things are not expedient: all things are lawful for me, but all things edify not." There are many behaviors that are simply not becoming of someone claiming to be a Christ follower. Although every possible behavior is not explicitly outlined in the Bible, our expected response and responsibility toward every action and behavior is. There are definite godly principles that are applicable to all actions and behaviors. The Bible is our guide to life, period. As believers, we cannot operate in this obscure "gray" area, and walk in the light.

The term "gray area," is located nowhere in the Word of God. The most closely related term to gray, is darkness. Man has created this category of thoughts and behaviors to justify actions that truly do not set us apart, or bring glory and honor to God. It is due to man's desire to be autonomous that we devise ways to justify behaviors and thoughts that really are out of alignment with God's will and desire for us. I Corinthians 6:12 says, "All things are lawful unto me, but all things are not expedient: all things are lawful for me, but I will not be brought under the power of any." This is not the freedom for which Christ went to the cross.

We are not free to dabble in sin, but we have been set free from the bondage of sin. Galatians 5:1 tells us, "Stand fast therefore in the liberty wherewith Christ hath made us free, and be not entangled again with the yoke of bondage." We are not free to do whatever our flesh, and the world wants for us. That puts us back in bondage. To call these "gray areas," is to grant our flesh too much authority.

Anything that we consider doing, or meditating on, that is not clearly addressed in scripture, should be filtered through the Word of God, and prayer. Psalm 119:105 tells us, "Thy word is a lamp unto my feet, and a light unto my path." There are no real gray areas if you filter everything through the lens of the Lord. After searching the Scripture, The Holy Spirit will guide you into all righteousness and truth. If you are walking in the light of the Lord, and not in rebellion, you will hear from the Holy Spirit.

It is when you have set in your mind what you want to do, that you are numb to the leading of the spirit into what actions will bring glory to God. John 1:5 tells us, "And the light shineth in darkness; and the darkness comprehended it not." When we allow our flesh to dictate our behavior, instead of the Holy Spirit, the results will never be God honoring. This is freedom, "Giving thanks unto the Father, which hath made us meet to be partakers of the inheritance of the saints in light: Who hath delivered us from the power of darkness, and hath translated us into the kingdom of his dear Son: In whom we have redemption through his blood, even the forgiveness of sins."(Colossians 1:12-14)

I Corinthians 10:31 says, "Whether therefore ye eat, or drink, or whatsoever ye do, do all to the glory of God." If whatever behavior you are engaging in fails to bring glory to God, it should be avoided. This is not legalism, but godliness. Many of the behaviors that people want to lump into this "gray area," would be difficult to do while simultaneously glorifying God.

There is no condemnation for those who walk after the Spirit. Romans 8:1-2 says, "There is therefore now no condemnation to them which are in Christ Jesus, who walk not after the flesh, but after the Spirit. For the law of the Spirit of life in Christ Jesus hath made me free from the law of sin and death." Christians tend to use this verse when they are clearly in rebellion, and trying to justify their conduct. This verse is not referring to someone who is walking in alignment with the flesh. Choose freedom in walking rightly with Jesus.

Finally, as sons and daughters of the King of Kings, we ought to desire a calling set apart from the world. Colossians 3:2 says, "Set your affections on things above, not on things on the earth." We use to be slaves to sin and the devil, but we forsook that life for the calling that the Lord placed on us.

Freedom is found in denying our flesh and its desires, and walking in newness of life. Romans 12:2 says, "And be not conformed to this world: but be ye transformed by the renewing of your mind, that ye may prove what is that good, and acceptable, and perfect, will of God."

It is a lie from the pit of hell that tells us that behaving similar to the standard of this world is okay for a Christ follower. I John 2:15-16 says, "Love not the world, neither the things that are in the world. If any man love the world, the love of the Father is not in him. For all that is in the world, the lust of the flesh, and the lust of the eyes, and the pride of life, is not of the Father, but is of the world." Choose to be set apart for God's glory.

Walk in Truth. Walk with clarity. Walk closely with Him who is worthy.

~Seek Godly Wisdom

There are tremendous benefits as a result of seeking Godly wisdom.

Everyone possesses a certain measure of "worldly wisdom," which is an understanding of the ways of the world that are not biblical in nature. Worldly wisdom is experience, knowledge, judgement, and understanding, that is qualified and measured by the standards of the world. I Corinthians 3:18-19 says, "Let no man deceive himself. If any man among you seemeth to be wise in this world, let him become a fool, that he may be wise. For the wisdom of this world is foolishness with God. For it is written, He taketh the wise in their own craftiness." God is saying that if we are deemed wise by the measure of the world, we should not boast in it. Worldly wisdom does not impress God.

Forsaking the wisdom of the world, and replacing it with Godly wisdom is what will produce a fruitful life. Worldly wisdom relies on our intellect, feelings, senses, and obtaining understanding from people, and the world. Worldly wisdom seeks understanding to profit self. Worldly wisdom is in large part self-serving. The wisdom we possess should boast of God, not of ourselves or the world. If wisdom isn't gained from God, and for God's purposes, it is worldly wisdom.

Worldly wisdom is obtained naturally, the longer we live on this earth. We all gain varying degrees of worldly wisdom. As a believer, the worldly wisdom that we possess, should be used to bring glory to God. Ephesians 4:14 warns, "That we henceforth be no more children, tossed to and fro, and carried about with every wind of doctrine, by the sleight of men, and cunning craftiness, whereby they lie in wait to deceive." We must align our worldly wisdom with the Word of God. If it does not align with the Word of God, it will not generate Kingdom benefits. If the worldly wisdom we possess cannot be used to bring glory to God, then it is of little use to us.

Beware of worldly wisdom that comes against the Word of God; it is of no use to those who follow the Lord. I Corinthians 1:19-20 tells us, "For it is written, I will destroy the wisdom of the wise, and will bring to nothing the understanding of the prudent. Where is the wise? where is the scribe? where is the disputer of this world? hath not God made foolish the wisdom of this world?" When we are full of worldly wisdom, it makes it more difficult to receive the Word of God with humility. Worldly wisdom has the potential to blind us to the will of God.

The manner in which we use or display the worldly wisdom that we possess, should reflect God's character in our personal, work, spiritual, and family lives. If it does not, reject it, and allow God to replace it. James 1:5 tells us, "If any of you lack wisdom, let him ask of God, that giveth to all men liberally, and upbraideth not; and it shall be given him."

We must seek after Godly wisdom. In I Kings, we learn about King Solomon. In I Kings 3:9 we learn that He asked God for wisdom when God said He would give him anything he asked for. God made him the wisest man to ever live. Over time, he ended up misusing the wisdom God gave him. He lacked humility. Proverbs 15:33 says, "The fear of the Lord is the instruction of wisdom; and before honour is humility." We want to seek Godly wisdom, but we must first seek God Himself. We should desire that God bless us with a spirit of humility, Godly wisdom, and discernment.

Godly wisdom comes directly from God. We are told in the book of James, how to detect Godly wisdom. There is evidence in Godly wisdom. James 3:17 says, "But the wisdom that is from above is first pure, then peaceable, gentle, [and] easy to be intreated, full of mercy and good fruits, without partiality, and without hypocrisy."

This is the evidence of Godly wisdom:

Godly wisdom is pure: It is pure, undivided, and free from anything evil. There is nothing unclean, corrupt, or carnal with Godly wisdom.

Godly wisdom is peaceable: It does not promote or produce conflict or offence. It is not contentious, but amicable and placid.

Godly wisdom is gentle: It is not harsh or severe, but kind and forbearing.

Godly wisdom is easily intreated: It is easily asked.

Godly wisdom is full of mercy: unmerited pardon and with good results

Godly wisdom is without partiality: not biased

Godly wisdom is without hypocrisy: honest and trustworthy

Proverbs 16:16 says, "How much better is it to get wisdom than gold! and get understanding rather to be chosen than silver!" It is good to desire Godly wisdom. Romans 11:33 says, "O the depth of the riches both of the wisdom and knowledge of God! how unsearchable are his judgments, and his ways past finding out!" Godly wisdom is profitable in every way, and keeps our eyes focused on the Lord.

Seek Godly wisdom.

~In Obedience, Choose Joy

God commands us to have joy. Let's experience the joy we have access to, and praise Him for it.

The words joy and rejoice are mentioned numerous times in the New and Old Testament. Joy is repeated some 167 times in the King James Version of the Old and New Testaments combined. The word rejoice is used in the King James Version around 248 times in the Old and New Testament together. These two words go hand in hand, and merit our attention, since they are both frequently woven into the pages of scripture.

There are many commands in Scripture, and surprisingly enough, we are also commanded to have joy. Yes, joy is a command. Philippians 4:4 commands, "Rejoice in the Lord always: and again I say, Rejoice." Rejoicing is defined as the act of expressing joy: the subject of joy. Interestingly, the definition of joy is to rejoice. Christ came to set captives (that is us) free.

As a result of being free, naturally we should be filled with joy. Psalm 149: 5 declares, "Let the saints be joyful in glory: let them sing aloud upon their beds." Rejoicing and having joy is a privilege. Isaiah 41:16 says rejoice because the Lord will scatter your enemies: "Thou shalt fan them, and the wind shall carry them away, and the whirlwind shall scatter them:

and thou shalt rejoice in the Lord, and shalt glory in the Holy One of Israel." We must have joy in our hearts, that overflows in our walk. Habakkuk 3:18 says, "Yet I will rejoice in the LORD, I will joy in the God of my salvation."

You might ask, "Is it possible to experience joy at all times?" With a resounding YES, we absolutely can have joy at all times. Joy and rejoicing can be present simultaneously with any of our other emotions. All throughout the Psalms we see joy parallel with other emotions, both positive and negative. For example, Psalm 126:5 reads," They that sow in tears shall reap in joy." As believers, we possess power, through The Holy Spirit of God, to experience joy inexplicable. In John 15:11, Paul writes, "These things have I spoken unto you, that my joy might remain in you, and that your joy might be full."

Emotions are generated based on our circumstances, whereas joy is not. Joy is constant, and it comes from God. It is an inner presence that dwells within. We can maintain a heart's posture of joy in the midst of any trial, disappointment, or tragedy. Romans 15:13 tells us, "Now the God of hope fill you with all joy and peace in believing, that ye may abound in hope, through the power of the Holy Ghost." We rejoice and are filled with joy due to our heart and mind being in alignment with God, through a personal relationship with Jesus Christ.

Joy is independent of happiness or any other emotion. Joy does not come or go based on your circumstances, but our emotions are dependent on the circumstances of life. Joy is our portion when we trust in The Lord. Joy is one of the fruits of the spirit. Galatians 5: 22-23 "But the fruit of the Spirit is love, joy, peace, longsuffering, gentleness, goodness, faith, Meekness, temperance: against such there is no law."

Joy is not only a command, but also a choice. Psalm 118:24 says, "This is the day which the Lord hath made; we will rejoice and be glad in it." We must choose to rejoice, and walk in joy. Psalm 71:23 shows that we are filled with joy because The Lord has saved us. "My lips shall greatly rejoice when I sing unto thee; and my soul, which thou hast redeemed."

Believe that you have received Joy, and that you can rejoice at all times. God has placed joy in His children. It is up to us to choose to walk in joy.

Choose joy each day.

~The Sovereignty of God: He Is In Control

It should bring us great peace and assurance to know that God is certainly in control. Regardless of what men declare, God is sovereign. Regardless of what any man says or does, God is sovereign. No one's opinion is going to impact the reality of the sovereignty of God. God is in control. Proverbs 16:9 says, "A man's heart deviseth his way: but the LORD directeth his steps."

Although it is true, God made us with free will, and we reap what we sow, He has ultimate control over all. Galatians 6:7 says, "Be not deceived; God is not mocked: for whatsoever a man soweth, that shall he also reap." Although it may be difficult to fully comprehend, be assured, that while man has free will, God remains in complete control of all things. He is sovereign over all His creation. Isaiah 14:24 tells us, "The LORD of hosts hath sworn, saying, Surely as I have thought, so shall it come to pass; and as I have purposed, so shall it stand."

For those of us who have placed our faith and trust in Almighty God, we must hold firmly to the truth that God is sovereign over all things. This should show forth in our approach toward any and all circumstances of life. This belief should impact our response to everything that occurs in our lives, and in the world. Psalm 22:28 says, "For the kingdom is the LORD'S: and he is the governor among the nations." God is sovereign: There is nothing outside of His control.

God not only permits certain occurrences and circumstances, but He also orders certain occurrences and circumstances. Everything that happens, falls under the authority of Almighty God. We are Christ's ambassadors, and He will guide our actions and our steps, so that we will represent Him well. We are not in control, He is.

We have assurance that everything, past; present; and future; is under God's control and rule. We must believe that nothing happens that has not been permitted, directed, or adjudicated by God. Ephesians 1:11 tells us, "In whom also we have obtained an inheritance, being predestinated according to the purpose of him who worketh all things after the counsel of his own will." God does not only work some things after the counsel of His will, but He works all things.

Although, we may not always fully comprehend the "why," we must understand that it is God's will that will always be fulfilled. In the midst of chaos, global turbulence, disaster, and all that is unthinkable, God is in control. We may not understand this side of heaven, but we must trust and believe in the sovereignty of God. We are not in control, He is.

Regardless of what is going on in our personal lives, God is sovereign. Despite the way the media portrays what is happening in our nation and the world, God is sovereign. In the midst of global unrest and societal dysfunction, God is sovereign. We must not lose sight of the sovereignty of God.

Before we allow our passions to get inflamed over conflict in our nation, recall the sovereignty of God. In the midst of the raging storms that we will encounter in our lives, remember God is in control, He is sovereign. Before we yield to our flesh, and unleash our outrage, and dissatisfaction, about anything going on in our world, remember God is not missing in action.

No, God is sovereign, and He is in control of every last detail, of everything that is good or bad. Isaiah 45:7 tells us, "I form the light, and create darkness: I make peace, and create evil: I the Lord do all these things." We are not in control, He is.

There is no authority greater than God's. There is nothing that is outside of God's control. There is no decision made by man, that is made without God's permission. No matter what is taking place in our lives, the lives of those we love, the world, our nation, our government, the media, etc. We must know beyond a shadow of a doubt, that God is sovereign.

Our purpose is to bring glory and honor to God, to represent Him well, to love, to show mercy and kindness, to extend grace, to pray for one another, to pray for our country, to pray for our leaders, to advocate without condemnation, and to trust and believe that God is sovereign. When the enemy tries to seduce us with His lies, we must cling to Truth. God is always in control.

Trust in the sovereignty of God.

~Keep Your Passion For Jesus Alive

When we initially place our faith and trust in Jesus Christ, there is humility, passion, hunger, and a zeal, that accompanies our transformation. When we realize who Jesus is, and what He has done for us, we come to Him like a child. Jesus desires us to be void of pride, and clothed in humility, just as a child.

Matthew 18:1-4 says, "At the same time came the disciples unto Jesus, saying, Who is the greatest in the kingdom of heaven? And Jesus called a little child unto him, and set him in the midst of them, And said, Verily I say unto you, Except ye be converted, and become as little children, ye shall not enter into the kingdom of heaven. Whosoever therefore shall humble himself as this little child, the same is greatest in the kingdom of heaven." Jesus does not suggest to be like a child; He says that we must be like a child. There are characteristics of children, that we must possess, and not lose, in order to fully receive all that the Lord has for us.

The type of child that Christ is instructing us to be, is humble; teachable; without pride; and able to trust. We lose a lot, if not all, of these characteristics as we approach adulthood. Christ calls us to return to our child-likeness, when we come to Him. He is clear when He says, "Except ye be converted, and become as little children, ye shall not enter into the kingdom of heaven. (Matthew 18:3)"

We must come to Christ with true vulnerability and hunger, desiring nothing else but to be in the presence of our Lord and Savior, Jesus Christ. God wants us to come to Him as a child, fully trusting in, and dependent on Him. II Corinthians 1:9 says, "But we had the sentence of death in ourselves, that we should not trust in ourselves, but in God which raiseth the dead." We cannot trust ourselves, but we can completely trust God. Let's never lose that faith, zeal, and trust that we possessed when we first yielded our lives to Christ.

We will not reach a moment, here on earth, when we will have learned all that God wants to teach us. Psalm 71:17 says, "O God, You have taught me from my youth, And I still declare Your wondrous deeds." We will not "arrive," to the maximum height of spirituality on this side of heaven. We will not exhaust all that Jesus desires to reveal to us through His Word and His ways. Let us maintain a passion for Christ. In Matthew 5:6, Jesus tells us, "Blessed are they which do hunger and thirst after righteousness: for they shall be filled." All the days that He blesses us with on this earth, should be spent drawing closer to Him, studying His Word, and boldly sharing the love of Christ with others.

I remember when I surrendered my all to Christ almost three decades ago. I literally could not get enough of the Word of God. I wanted to study the Bible all the time, and I shared Jesus with anyone who would listen. I was not ashamed, and I was excited about my relationship with Jesus. I wanted to be under good spiritual leadership, and I was eager to be taught. I possessed great passion and zeal, because Jesus changed me.

My life was completely renewed, and I wanted everyone to know why. I was a child again, a child of the King of Kings.

After about fifteen years, I began to settle in, and I lost that passion that I had. I got comfortable, and I became complacent. This is not a place we want to be. God began to show me that He never wants us to lose the hunger, the passion, and the desire for more of Him in our lives. He revived within me the passion and desire that I previously had for so many years.

We must continue on with passion and hunger, sharing Jesus, and growing in our walk with Him. We will never be perfected here on earth, but we will be a work in progress. Look at Paul, as he recognized that while we are still on this earth, we will not attain perfection, and we have plenty to learn from Jesus. Our main goal should be to become more like Christ. In Philippians 3:12, Paul says, "Not as though I had already attained, either were already perfect: but I follow after, if that I may apprehend that for which also I am apprehended of Christ Jesus."

The more we desire Christ in us, the more transparent and passionate we become. Always desire to grow deeper in your walk with the Lord. Maintain the zeal and appetite for God's Word and fellowship with Jesus. Finally, as long as you have a breath to breathe; share your faith. Watch and see how your relationship with Jesus will flourish. Maintain your passion.

~Refiner's Fire

A refiner, or craftsman, restores things to its intended purpose or beauty. A refiner accomplishes this refining process with the use of fire. The continual process of purifying through refining fire, produces a purer, more restored, substance. Scripture refers to the refining of silver, illustrating how God refines us, His children.

God is our craftsman, our refiner. Job 23:10 says, "But he knoweth the way that I take: [when] he hath tried me, I shall come forth as gold." We are sanctified, or made holy in His sight, through His refining fire.

I am reminded of a story often told about a craftsman explaining the refining process to a curious observer, who had been studying the Book of Malachi in the Bible. He told her that when refining silver, the craftsman has to hold the silver in the middle of the fire, because it is the hottest part of the flame. This is done in order that all the impurities will burn off. So that all of the imperfections will be removed.

She recalled the Bible verses in Malachi, where it talks about refining fire. Malachi 3:2-3 says, "But who may abide the day of his coming? And who shall stand when he appeareth? For he is like a refiner's fire, and like fullers' soap: And he shall sit as a refiner and purifier of silver: and he shall purify the sons of Levi, and purge them as gold and silver, that they may offer unto the Lord an offering in righteousness." God is like a refiner's fire.

Psalm 51:10 says, "Create in me a clean heart, O God; and renew a right spirit within me."

She asked the craftsman if he was literally required to sit there throughout the entire process of refinement. He told her, "Yes, I must keep my gaze fixed on the silver the entire time. If I fail to remove the silver from the fire, even a moment too late, the silver will be ruined.

The woman thought about this tedious process, and asked him how he knew the appropriate time to remove the silver from under the hot flames. He answered her, and said, "I know to remove the silver from the flame, when I am able to see my reflection in it." This is perfectly aligned with what happens to us, as God molds us into the men and women of God that He desires us to be.

He desires to see His reflection, when He looks at us. He desires that as we grow in our understanding and love of our Lord and Savior, Jesus Christ, we will be transformed. We will look more and more like Him, we will be a reflection of His love, grace, and mercy. We will be more and more like Jesus, as God refines us. God is the refiner, and we are the silver.

~How God Refines Us

When we first come to the knowledge of the saving power of Jesus Christ, we are dirty, wrought with sin, and full of impurities and misgivings. God, through the miracle-working, life-changing power of His Holy Spirit, begins the refining process of our hearts and minds. This refining process lasts until we get to heaven one day in our perfected state. He refines us through the fire of experience, trials, temptations, and His Truth, which is the Word of God.

God uses every experience and trial that we go through. Nothing that we go through is endured in vain. God will use it for His glory. He is molding and shaping us, as we go through the fires of life. He is the refiner. I Peter 1:7 says, "That the trial of your faith, being much more precious than of gold that perisheth, though it be tried with fire, might be found unto praise and honor and glory at the appearing of Jesus Christ." Jesus refines us.

It is through our trials that we learn obedience, and authentic surrender. It is through our trials, that our faith and dependence on Jesus is strengthened. As we go through the trials of life, He removes the impurities, and anything that does not bring glory to His name. He strengthens us as a result of our perseverance through the storms of life. Isaiah

48:10 says, "Behold, I have refined thee, but not with silver; I have chosen thee in the furnace of affliction." Jesus refines us.

It is through the testing of our faith, through trials, and life experiences, that Christ is making us more like Him. Just like the craftsman, Jesus pulls us from the fire at the perfect time. John 16:33 tells us, "These things I have spoken unto you, that in me ye might have peace. In the world ye shall have tribulation: but be of good cheer; I have overcome the world." The Holy Spirit guides us through the trials and the circumstances of life that test our faith, if we place our faith and trust in Him. Jesus refines us.

God refines us as we resist the temptations that we face. God refines us through adversity. He refines us as we stand in the middle of the fire. I Corinthians 10:13 says, "There hath no temptation taken you but such as is common to man: but God [is] faithful, who will not suffer you to be tempted above that ye are able; but will with the temptation also make a way to escape, that ye may be able to bear [it]." The Holy Spirit is with us, and will help us escape the lure of every temptation we face, if we trust in Him. The Holy Spirit will offer a way of escape when we are tempted by the things of this world. He will pull us out of the fire, at the perfect time, if we are walking in obedience to Him. Jesus refines us.

As we continue to yield to The Holy Spirit, He will refine us, and we will look more and more like Him. I Peter 1:6-7 says, "Wherein ye greatly rejoice, though now for a season, if need be, ye are in heaviness through manifold temptations: That the trial of your faith, being much more precious than of gold that perisheth, though it be tried with fire, might be found unto praise and honour and glory at the appearing of Jesus Christ:" Jesus refines us.

Oftentimes, God will use His Word to refine our walk with Jesus. He uses His perfect, irrefutable Word as the fire, as He refines us. God will show us the people, behaviors, thoughts, entertainment, activities, and consumption, to convict our hearts of what needs to be brought back into alignment with His will. He will illuminate Scripture, that speaks to the refining He is doing. Jesus refines us.

God is always in the process of refining us. Just as the craftsman repeats the refining process over and over, so it is with God. Proverbs 17:3 says, "The fining pot is for silver, and the furnace for gold: but the LORD trieth the hearts." He is continually removing from our lives anything that does not reflect His image. I Peter 5:10 says, "But the God of all grace, who hath called us unto his eternal glory by Christ Jesus, after that ye have suffered a while, make you perfect, stablish, strengthen, settle you." God is like a refiner's fire.

It is truly our choice as to how refined we become. If we resist the Holy Spirit who convicts, convinces, and refines, we will remain a version of who we used to be. This is not where God wants us. There is freedom in the refining. Although, we may go through much pain, the transformation on the other side, is worth it. Allow Jesus to refine you.

~Do You Want Jesus To Direct Your Path?

Let's look at a verse from Proverbs, that is one of the most widely used verses for encouragement in times of vulnerability, uncertainty, confusion, and doubt.

Proverbs 3:5-6 says, "Trust in the LORD with all thine heart; and lean not unto thine own understanding. In all thy ways acknowledge him, and he shall direct thy paths." These verses end with a promise, but begin with prerequisites to the promise being fulfilled.

God desires to direct our paths, and He desires to bless our lives. In order for God to do these things, we have to submit to His will. We must rid ourselves of disbelief, and believe that God loves us, and has our best interests at heart. When we truly believe, it is easier to trust and surrender our all to the Lord.

In order for the Lord to direct our path, we must trust in Him with our whole heart. Jeremiah 17:7 says, "Blessed is the man that trusteth in the LORD, and whose hope the LORD is" As Christ followers, if we fail to place our trust in the Lord, we will have no peace, power, security, or hope. We can trust God, because His Word is completely true. He is trustworthy. He never changes. We do not have to worry about God changing with cultural trends or popular ideas of the times.

Hebrews 13:8 tells us, "Jesus Christ the same yesterday, today, and forever."

We can trust the Lord because He is love. I John 4:16 says, "And we have known and believed the love that God hath to us. God is love; and he that dwelleth in love dwelleth in God, and God in him." In order to authentically trust the Lord, we must get to know Him through studying His Word, and prayer. We must be in fellowship with the Lord. It is impossible to truly trust someone who we do not know. In John 17:3, Jesus says, "And this is life eternal, that they might know thee the only true God, and Jesus Christ, whom thou hast sent." The more we know Him, the more we will depend on Him, and our trust deepens.

In order for the Lord to direct our path, we must "lean not on our own understanding." Not leaning on our own understanding means that we recognize our limited ability to understand the ways of God. We accept that His ways are higher than ours, and we must rely on The Lord to fill us with His understanding. God is always right, He is truth. He will never steer us wrong, nor will He ever lie. We can depend on our Lord and Savior, Jesus Christ. We must lean on Jesus for understanding, because our understanding is tainted by sin, our flesh, and the world.

Isaiah 55: 8-9 tells us, "For my thoughts are not your thoughts, neither are your ways my ways, saith the Lord. For as the heavens are higher than the earth, so are my ways higher than your ways, and my thoughts than your thoughts." Our understanding is limited, and we are unable to see the big picture of things. God has a panoramic view. We do not have the breadth of understanding and insight that God does. He is omniscient, and He knows all things. There is nothing beyond His understanding. When we trust in Him, His understanding will manifest in and through us.

In order for the Lord to direct our path, we must acknowledge Him in all our ways. I John 4: 15 says, "Whosoever shall confess that Jesus is the Son of God, God dwelleth in him, and he in God." We cannot partially obey the Lord. We can not only invite Him into parts of our lives. He is an all or none God. We must relinquish autonomy in our lives, and give God all authority.

We must recognize, and approve of His Lordship in our lives. Acknowledging God in every aspect of our lives, both publicly and privately, is what the Lord desires of us, as expressed in this verse. This is necessary in our walk with the Lord. Hebrews 10:23 says, "Let us hold fast the profession of our faith without wavering; for he is faithful that promised."

Let's commit to allowing Almighty God, through the power of His Holy Spirit to manifest Himself in every area of our lives. Allow Him to take hold of us, and direct our paths. His desire is that we will yield to the Spirit of God. God is God, and there is nothing too big or little for Him. If we read God's Word closely, for truth and understanding, we will notice that many of God's promises require our obedience. Let's make it our ambition, to walk in obedience to Christ.

~Praying God's Will And His Word

I John 5:14-15 tells us, "And this is the confidence that we have in him, that, if we ask anything according to his will, he heareth us: And if we know that he hear us, whatsoever we ask, we know that we have the petitions that we desired of him." God's will is His desire, His plan, His purpose, or what He has determined. Additionally, God's will can never contradict His Word.

"If we ask according to His will, He hears us." When we pray, we must make certain that what we are praying aligns with God's desires, plans, and purpose. In order to pray in this way, we must know Him, and His Word. In order for us to know His Word, we must read and study His Word. It is then, that He hears our prayers. We are God's children, saved by the blood of His son, Jesus Christ. The Father hears His children.

I John 5:15 says, "And if we know that He hears us, whatsoever we ask, we know that we have the petitions that we desired of Him." If we pray God's desire, what we have prayed, will be. This can be difficult to fully understand. If we have prayed according to His will, it is done, or it will be done eventually. If what we have prayed never comes to pass, it was not His will, or it was not what He had determined.

God does what He has determined to do. He is sovereign. He is in control of all things. Ephesians 1:11 says, "In whom also we have obtained an inheritance, being predestinated according to the purpose of him who worketh all things after the counsel of his own will." Because of this, when we pray we must know that the outcome is God's will. God's will, not ours, is always what God will do.

In Matthew 6:10 of the Lord's prayer we hear Jesus say, "Thy kingdom come, Thy will be done in earth, as it is in heaven." Because we do not always know the explicit will of God for everything we ask, we say, "not my will, but Yours be done."

John 15:7 says, 'If ye abide in me, and my words abide in you, ye shall ask what ye will, and it shall be done unto you." We can look to the Bible, the Word of God, to know what we should be praying for.

The things that we pray that are not explicitly written in God's Word, should align with His will, character, principles, and His purposes. When we read God's Word, we should write down all references to prayer, and God's will, and incorporate them into our prayer life.

As we read our Bible, there are countless passages that tell us what to pray. For example, Matthew 26:41 tells us, "Watch and pray, that ye enter not into temptation: the spirit indeed is willing, but the flesh is weak." Therefore, we should be praying that we resist temptation, obey the spirit, and deny our flesh.

We must pray for all men, and our leaders. In I Timothy 2:1-2, we are told , "I exhort therefore, that, first of all, supplications, prayers, intercessions, and giving of thanks, be made for all men; for kings, and for all that are in authority; that we may lead a quiet and peaceable life in all godliness and honesty." If God tells us to pray for it in scripture, it is best to earnestly pray for those things when we pray.

As we read our Bible, there are countless passages that express God's will for our lives. For example, Romans 12:2 says, "And be not conformed to this world: but be ye transformed by the renewing of your mind, that ye may prove what is that good, and acceptable, and perfect, will of God." Another example is found in Ephesians 4:29 when it says, "Let no corrupt communication proceed out of your mouth, but that which is good to the use of edifying, that it may minister grace unto the hearers." Praying God's will, as expressed in Scripture, is an awesome way to pray. It is also a great way to learn God's Word.

Finally, as it is written in I Thessalonians 5:17-18, "Pray without ceasing. In everything give thanks: for this is the will of God in Christ Jesus concerning you." So, dearly loved by God, keep praying, and give God thanks in all things. Come to God in prayer, with confidence and devotion. Hebrews 4:16 tells us, "Let us therefore come boldly unto the throne of grace, that we may obtain mercy, and find grace to help in time of need."

Spend time in prayer, and watch how God answers. It may be with a "yes," it may be "no," or it may be "wait." Take note of God's faithfulness, and how "all things work together for good to them that love God, to them who are the called according to his purpose." (Romans 8:28).

~Finally, Put On Your Armor

We must not be found without our armor. Ephesians 6:11. It says, "Put on the whole armour of God, that ye may be able to stand against the wiles of the devil." It is important to understand that Ephesians 6:11 will only prove to be effective if we do what it says. We will be found ill equipped, ineffective, and defeated, if we fail to do our required part. In order to be able to stand against the wiles, schemes, ruses, and craftiness, of the devil, we must put on the full armor of God.

Ephesians 6:12 explains exactly who our battle is against. It declares, "For we wrestle not against flesh and blood, but against principalities, against powers, against the rulers of the darkness of this world, against spiritual wickedness in high places."

It is imperative that we are well informed warriors. We need a proper understanding of who we are in battle against. We are not engaged in combat with human beings. Our battle is not against anyone in our earthly lives. We are not in battle with our spouse, family member, government leaders or entities, co-workers, liberals, conservatives, people with ungodly agendas, ourselves, our situations, our past, or any other thing. Our battle, our struggle is with the unseen demonic forces in the spirit realm.

Our foe that we are at war with is dangerous, and encompasses many levels. He lurks within the unseen places in the heavenlies. Make no mistake, and please do not downplay the power that the devil has to steal, kill, manipulate, and destroy. God remains much more powerful than Satan, and He has already won the battle. Although, the battle was won at Calvary, Satan and the other fallen angels are wreaking havoc in the lives of believers. Prior to being eternally cast into the lake of fire, the devil was an angelic being. He rebelled against God, and was thrust out of heaven. He has been causing trouble ever since. We must be prepared, and equipped for battle.

Ephesians 6:13 tells us, "Wherefore take unto you the whole armour of God, that ye may be able to withstand in the evil day, and having done all, to stand."

We are told that we must do something, to see the result. If we take unto ourselves the whole armor, we will be able to withstand in the evil day. We are commanded to take up the "whole" armor. Clearly, this is all we need to stand, but we need all of it. A partial suit of armor will not suffice. Withstand means to remain undamaged, unaffected by, to resist, or to stand up against with resolve. The text says "may be able to withstand," because it is contingent on us taking up the full armor. When we take up the entire armor, we will be able to withstand and stand.

Ephesians 6: 13-18 tells us exactly what each piece of the Armor of God is. We need to understand what it means to put on the full Armor of God, in readiness for battle. We put on the first three pieces of the Armor of God permanently, and we are ready for battle. The next four pieces, we "take." In taking, there is ongoing, consistent action involved constantly, on the part of the believer. We are in a very real battle, on the front lines.

272

We are to be standing, dressed, and ready with our loins girt about with truth, our breastplate of righteousness on, and our feet shod with the preparation of the gospel of peace. These parts of the armor, are fixed, and in place. We do not take them off and put them back on, every time the enemy engages us in battle. Remember, we cannot physically see our enemy unless he is using someone or something to fulfill his purposes. Even then, he is sneaky. There isn't a label attached to whom or what is being used by him that says, "Hey, I am being used by Satan to lie, steal, deceive, and destroy you."

Ephesians 6: 14-15 commands, "Stand therefore, having your loins girt about with truth, and having on the breastplate of righteousness; And your feet shod with the preparation of the gospel of peace."

We must Stand with our loins girt about with Truth with the Breastplate of Righteousness in place. We must maintain our posture of strength and resolve while standing. First, we must have on the belt of truth, God's Truth. God's truth must be permanently wrapped around you.

In preparation for mobility in battle, the ancient Hebrews would have to lift their tunics between their legs, and tuck them into, or tie around, the central region of their body. Instead of a tunic, our loins must be girted with God's Truth. Next, we must permanently wear the breastplate of righteousness. We must be protected by righteousness. We must walk in right standing with God and His Word, not giving way to our flesh. Confess our sin, repent, and keep our walk blameless.

We must keep our hearts stayed on Christ, walking according to God's will not our own. This is how we are adorned with the breastplate of righteousness. Thirdly, we must have on our spiritual shoes. Roman soldiers had nails or spikes on the bottoms of their shoes to hold them to the ground. We are to have a firm stance in and on the gospel of peace. Our firmly positioned feet are prepared, and ready in the gospel of Jesus Christ which brings peace.

The gospel offers peace, even during battle. Now we are suited with the parts of the armor that are never removed. Galatians 5:1 tells us, "Stand fast therefore in the liberty wherewith Christ hath made us free, and be not entangled again with the yoke of bondage." Now stand, knowing these first three parts of your armor are fixed upon you.

Ephesians 6: 16-18 requires quick action in the midst of battle. "Above all, taking the shield of faith, wherewith ye shall be able to quench all the fiery darts of the wicked. And take the helmet of salvation, and the sword of the Spirit, which is the word of God: Praying always with all prayer and supplication in the Spirit, and watching thereunto with all perseverance and supplication for all saints."

Take up the shield of faith. The Roman soldiers had different types of shields, but I believe Paul was referring to the massive shields they used in battle. A Roman Soldier's shield was large, and covered them completely. They would create a wall of protection with them. This wall of shields would protect them from the fiery darts. We must walk closely with the Lord, and our faith in Him must be sure.

Hebrews 11:1 tells us, "Now faith is the substance of things hoped for, and the evidence of things not seen." Romans 10:17 tells us, "So then faith cometh by hearing, and hearing by the word of God." Having faith is believing God. Faith is believing. Take up, and stand behind your belief. I Corinthians 2:5 says, "That your faith should not stand in the wisdom of men, but in the power of God," This faith, this belief, will quench all the fiery darts of the wicked. Go, take up your shield of faith.

Take the helmet of salvation. The helmet protects our head and our mind. Because of God's grace and mercy, He has offered us the free gift of salvation if we believe, and receive it. The helmet protects us from the lies, accusations, and deception of the devil. I Thessalonians 5:8-9 tells us, "But let us, who are of the day, be sober, putting on the breastplate of faith and love; and for an helmet, the hope of salvation. For God hath not appointed us to wrath, but to obtain salvation by our Lord Jesus Christ," Place your faith and trust in Jesus Christ, and take up your helmet of Salvation.

We must take the Sword of the Spirit: The Word of God. Hebrews 4:12 says, "For the word of God is quick, and powerful, and sharper than any two-edged sword, piercing even to the dividing asunder of soul and spirit, and of the joints and marrow, and is a discerner of the thoughts and intents of the heart." Know the Word, and place it in your heart. Psalm 119:11 says, "Thy word have I hid in mine heart, that I might not sin against thee." Stay in The Word of God. This is how we understand God and His ways. We must immerse ourselves in His Word, written for us. We must be able to use the Word as our weapon at any moment in battle.

Lastly, pray. Be always in fellowship with our God and Savior, through prayer. 1 Thessalonians 5:17 tells us, "Pray without ceasing."

You know the love of God that reigns in your heart. Your heart and mind are stayed on Christ. You are a diligent student of the Word and prayer. You are victorious because of Jesus. You are fully equipped.

~Afterward

Thank you, for taking the time to read "Our Path For His Glory." I pray that the studies throughout this book helped you in your walk with the Lord. I pray that you recognize the need to keep your heart and mind stayed on Jesus. Knowing Jesus involves knowing His Word and His ways. My desire for you is to know God, and the power of His Holy Spirit. If I accomplished one thing, which is giving you some tools to know Jesus better, then I have succeeded.

Be encouraged in your journey with Jesus. There is no better place to be, than in the presence of the Lord. Enjoy your walk with Him, and come back to these readings from time to time, for encouragement and hope. Keep God in His proper place in your life, and all will be well with you. No matter what comes your way, you are more than a conqueror, in Jesus' name. Be blessed, and be a blessing. Be encouraged, and be an encourager. Be hopeful, and offer hope to others. Finally, walk in belief, righteousness, and understanding.

Kimmy Kay

Made in the USA
Monee, IL
16 January 2020

20436141R00157